THE JONAH FACTOR ®

THE JONAH FACTOR®

13 Spiritual Steps
to Finding the Job of a Lifetime

Ed Klodt

MINNEAPOLIS

THE JONAH FACTOR®
13 Spiritual Steps to Finding the Job of a Lifetime

Copyright © 2006 Ed Klodt. All rights reserved. Except for brief quotations in critical articles or reviews, no part of this book may be reproduced in any manner without prior written permission from the publisher. Visit www.augsburgfortress.org/copyrights/contact. asp or write to Permissions, Augsburg Fortress, Publishers, Box 1209, Minneapolis, MN 55440-1209.

Large-quantity purchases or custom editions of this book are available at a discount from the publisher. For more information, contact the sales department at Augsburg Fortress, Publishers, 1-800-328-4648, or write to: Sales Director, Augsburg Fortress, Publishers, Box 1209, Minneapolis, MN 55440-1209.

Scripture quotations, unless otherwise marked, are taken from the Holy Bible, New International Version®. Copyright© 1973, 1978, 1984 by International Bible Society. Used by permission of Zondervan. All rights reserved.

Scripture passages marked NRSV are from the New Revised Standard Version of the Bible, copyright © 1946, 1952, 1971, 1989 by the Division of Christian Education of the National Council of the Churches of Christ in the USA. Used by permission.

Visit www.jonahfactor.com for more information or contact the author at:
The Jonah Factor®
1534 North Moorpark Road, #118
Thousand Oaks, CA 91360-5129

Library of Congress Cataloging-in-Publication Data
Klodt, Ed, 1953-
The Jonah factor : 13 spiritual steps to finding the job of a lifetime / Ed Klodt.
p. cm.
Includes bibliographical references and index.
ISBN-13: 978-0-8066-5617-5
ISBN-10: 0-8066-5617-4 (pbk. : alk. paper)
1. Bible. O.T. Jonah—Criticism, interpretation, etc. 2. Job hunting—Religious aspects—Christianity. 3. Work—Religious aspects—Christianity. 4. Vocation—Christianity. I. Title.
BS1605.6.W735K56 2006
248.8'8—dc22 2006008495

Cover design by Laurie Ingram; Cover photo © Fotosearch. Used by permission.
Book design by Michelle L. N. Cook

The paper used in this publication meets the minimum requirements of American National Standard for Information Sciences—Permanence of Paper for Printed Library Materials, ANSI Z329.48-1984. ♾ ™

Manufactured in the United States of America.

10   09   08   07   06   1   2   3   4   5   6   7   8   9   10

To Lyn,

who embraced

the adventure

Contents

Introduction

Two roads diverged in a wood, and I—

I took the one less traveled by,

And that has made all the difference.

—*Robert Frost,* The Road Not Taken

MOST OF US DON'T WANT TO BE AT WORK.

While on the job, we daydream about weekends, vacations, and even retirement. We imagine ourselves in different careers with different responsibilities working with different people at other companies. An occupation that once was interesting—or at least bearable—is now burdensome. And, with many of us working an increasing number of hours each week, we're spending more time engaged in what feels like dead-end activities.

Even when we're not on the job, we dread the start of another workweek. Our anxiety starts with malaise on Sunday afternoon as we think about the week ahead, swells into mild depression that evening, and then reaches its peak on Monday morning. The cycle is repeated each week as we gird ourselves to work at jobs we tolerate, at best, or hate, at worst. Perhaps that's why more heart attacks and strokes occur on Monday mornings than at any other time.

Workplace misery is common, and it's destructive. It fuels the purchase of lottery tickets, strains marriages, and contributes to alcoholism. More than half of American workers say they are dissatisfied with their jobs, many of them miserably so. We see them in our workplaces, schools, government offices, and churches. Perhaps we even stare at them in the mirror getting ready for work each weekday morning.

This dissatisfaction extends into the ranks of the retiree, the stay-at-home parent, the student, the community volunteer, and even those involved in full-time ministry as they engage in activities, studies, and tasks that they no longer enjoy.

How did it come to this? In the United States, this fabled land of limitless opportunity, why does one out of every four working Americans stay on the job merely to earn a paycheck? What happened to the joy and fulfillment that's supposed to be part of our life's work? In all likelihood, we suffer from the same misery that befell Jonah the prophet: We're not doing what God has called us to do, and we pay a very heavy price for it.

I was a Jonah for much of my adult life, trying to dodge God and his plans for me. I thought I could outrun—or at least outlast—God. It wasn't until fairly recently that I finally let go of my nearsighted plans and let God direct me into the work I was created to do. Within the years-long struggle that led to my decision to "LET GO and LET GOD" is the story of *The Jonah Factor*®.

I had known for a long time that God was prompting me to do something different with my life. However, like Jonah, I resisted God's prodding to change course. Eventually, God captured my attention and set me on the remarkable path I'm now on. Doing so required my obedience and a willingness to take a big risk—not easy for this hardheaded, painfully practical son of German immigrants.

My Dream Job Became a Burden

Let me share some background: For almost thirty years I had been a manager of sales, marketing, and internal communications departments at several large corporations, advancing to a fairly senior position at an international investment management firm. It was a dream job in many ways, the culmination of decades of hard work and sacrifice. I enjoyed financial success I had never imagined, was rewarded with growing responsibilities, and basked in the ego gratification that comes from frequent promotions and corporate officer titles.

Yet, I grew progressively unhappy. Increasingly, my generous salary, corporate perks, and upper-middle-class lifestyle weren't sufficient to drown out the growing sense that I was lost. Rising before five o'clock each workday morning became more and more burdensome. My two-and-a-half-hour daily commute, on top of ten- to twelve-hour workdays, went from stimulating to bearable to excruciating. As time progressed, I resented my wife and children because, as sole income earner for the family, I was running this gauntlet every weekday to pay the mortgage, buy the groceries, and maintain our very comfortable living standard.

I should have loved my job. In the waning days of my corporate career, I worked for an outstanding organization whose scrupulously ethical practices and principled people were a pleasure to work with. I had a talented staff (truly the best in the business), bosses who appreciated and rewarded me, and a job that, in spite of my responsibilities to run our national sales campaigns, didn't require me to travel much. My plan was to retire from this firm, taking an early retirement, if possible.

However, my discontent grew as I felt a growing urgency to move on, to do something very different with my life. That strong sense came from a variety of sources, some human and others spiritual. I increasingly heard God's voice telling me, *"It's over. This is not what I created you to do. Listen. I have other plans."* At one point, almost every Scripture verse I read, sermon I heard, and prayer time encounter I had with God seemed to prod me to leave my job, trusting that God would take care of me. Over time this message grew in urgency and in volume. As if to validate that sense, volunteer work I was doing to serve God through my church and elsewhere gave me great joy and fulfillment.

However, I faced a variety of seemingly insurmountable obstacles, prompting such troublesome questions as: Where was God leading me? Was it really God prompting me to move on—or simply the proverbial midlife crisis I had so far escaped? How would I pay the bills if I left my job, including college expenses for our two teenagers, one of whom was already in college and for whom we were paying full tuition? Would people think I had lost my mind, leaving an excellent job working for an outstanding company?

Discerning God's Call

This book grew out of my struggle with God regarding the future. The 13 Steps of discernment I developed during this intense period are what guided me and allowed me to hear the Lord's voice more clearly and to feel confident that the steps I was taking were, indeed, a stairway God had set before me.

These steps, which I've called *The Jonah Factor*®, have redirected me from a life of growing desperation to one in which every day has been a blessing and an adventure, exactly as God has intended. Family members and longtime friends now remark that I seem like a new man. And isn't that exactly the business God is in—turning each of us into "a new creation" (2 Corinthians 5:17)?

The Jonah Factor can be your tool for discerning God's call, to help you experience the joy that has escaped you, and to lead you toward a rich life in harmony with what God created you to do.

There is a specific call to work that God has placed on your life. It's explicitly for you, and God has given you the talents, time, strength and financial resources to discover it. Embrace it and you'll have the abundant life Jesus promised when he said, "I have come that they may have life, and have it to the full" (John 10:10). Be prepared to give up all control and surrender yourself to God's plans. That will require a leap of faith. Trust God and don't worry. God is faithful.

Is God calling you to do something different with your life? If you're like a growing number of Americans, there's a strong likelihood you're stuck in a spiral similar to the one I was in. Perhaps God is prompting you toward something new, whispering, "See, I am doing a new thing! Now it springs up; do you not perceive it?" (Isaiah 43:19).

This book isn't really the story of Jonah. More than likely it's the story of you.

After all, there's a little bit of Jonah in all of us.

—*Ed Klodt*
Thousand Oaks, California

Part One

· · · · · · · · · · · · · · ·

Working in the
21st Century

Men for the sake of getting a living forget to live.

—*Margaret Fuller*

I looked at the wall clock: 25 minutes until lunch,

30 minutes for lunch, then 5 more hours plus 2 hours overtime,

an hour to drive home, ten minutes to bathe, 30 minutes to eat,

20 minutes to read the paper and in another hour you'd be asleep,

only to wake up in the morning, dress, get a quick coffee,

then an hour to drive back in plus half-a-day on Saturday

and then back on Monday.

—*Charles Bukowski,* Slouching Toward Nirvana

CHAPTER ONE

The Perfect Storm

When work is a pleasure, life is a joy!

When work is a duty, life is slavery.

—*Maxim Gorky*

THE AMERICAN WORKER IS ABOUT TO BE HIT BY THE PERFECT STORM. In fact, its leading edge is already on the radar. The cold fronts of demographics, life expectancy, consumerism, savings rates, retirement, and job satisfaction are about to collide, threatening to rob us of the joy and satisfaction we seek now, or at least hope will be ours later in life.

As a growing wave of baby boomers looks ahead to retirement, there's an increasing realization that most of us will have to remain employed longer than we had envisioned, trapped in jobs we enjoy less and less. Increasingly, we'll have to stretch our countdown to retirement, perhaps considerably.

At the same time, our lifestyles have placed us in bondage. They lock us into working to pay the bills and to put away enough money to fund the retirements we see as salvation from jobs for which we no longer have a passion. Plus, our increasingly secular viewpoint of work denies God an opportunity to guide us into jobs, careers, and even volunteer activities that will bring us the joy and fulfillment God intends.

Most of us will be required to work for more years—perhaps many more—than we want to. Because of ill-advised lifestyle choices, statistical happenstance, and plain-old human inertia, we'll remain at jobs for which we have little enthusiasm, many of us into our late sixties and early seventies, according to a growing body of evidence.

Let's look more closely at the storm clouds on the horizon.

Demographics: We'll Be Expected to Work Later in Life

Baby boomers (those born between 1946 and 1964) are nearing retirement in record numbers. Seven Americans turn fifty every minute, a trend expected to continue until 2014, according to *American Demographics* magazine.

Today's fifty-year-old bears little resemblance to someone born a century ago. In 1901, life expectancy at birth was forty-nine years. The average American born at the turn of the twentieth century wouldn't even have celebrated his or her fiftieth birthday. Life expectancy in the United States has increased more than 50 percent since then, climbing to a record 77.6 years in 2003, according to the United States Centers for Disease Control and Prevention. Today's fifty-year-old can expect to live even longer. Data shows that the average fifty-year-old American will live another thirty-three years, almost two decades past the traditional retirement age of sixty-five.

Today's pre-retiree is also stronger and healthier than his predecessors, negating one of the historical reasons for retiring at sixty-five. In addition, fewer people today work at the physically demanding jobs that employed their parents and grandparents.

Automation and other productivity enhancements increasingly put people at desks or on sales floors instead of assembly lines and scaffolds. There's a growing expectation that people will work later in life because they're more physically fit and jobs are less rigorous.

Even without being compelled to retire at age sixty-five, Americans are already rethinking their golden years. In fact, there's an emergent trend of retirement-aged people starting second careers a few years after they've gotten their fill of travel, hobbies, and spoiling the grandkids. A survey in 2004 by Plansponsor.com indicates that 74 percent of workers plan to work at least part-time during retirement.

The federal government is also zeroing in on the trend for people to work longer, whether by choice or necessity. Among the more often-cited proposals to fix Social Security are those that would increase the age at which Americans can begin tapping into those benefits. In fact, what Social Security considers the "full retirement age" is no longer sixty-five. It's been bumped up to sixty-six years, with further increases almost certain in the years to come.

American business, too, is changing its thinking regarding older workers. Whereas companies often jettisoned longtime employees in favor of more flexible and less highly compensated workers, efforts are growing to keep experienced people on the payroll instead of putting them out to pasture. That sea change isn't because corporations have suddenly developed a warm spot in their hearts for older workers. Simple demographics are prompting it.

In 1960, 9.2 percent of the United States population was sixty-five or older. By 2000, that figure had increased to 12.4 percent. By 2025, fully 18.5 percent of Americans—sixty-two-million people—will be sixty-five or older, according to the Bureau of the Census. And there aren't enough workers coming up behind them to fill positions vacated as they head for retirement. This trend is expected to erupt as rising numbers of boomers, especially white-collar workers, near retirement.

In fact, a 2005 International Monetary Fund study estimated that resolving this age crisis in much of the developed world by 2050 will require either an 11 percent increase in the number of people who work, a 30 percent immigration increase into countries like the United States, or raising the "traditional" retirement age by seven years.

All of those statistics point to the need to keep Americans in the workforce longer, whether by choice or necessity.

Ironically, that development could be a blessing in disguise for the growing number of Americans who will have insufficient financial resources to leave their jobs at age sixty-five.

Savings Rates: We're Going to Have to Work Longer

Here's a news flash: Americans are lousy savers. That's been well established for decades. However, it has gotten far worse in recent years.

The reasons are as varied as the individuals behind the statistics. Some of us are simply spendthrifts who don't control our desires for more and more stuff. Others are caught in a vise of growing expenses we truly can't control. This group includes members of the "sandwich generation" who are wedged between the responsibilities of raising children and putting them through college while at the same time having to take care of aging parents.

For those and other reasons, personal savings rates have plummeted in recent years. Continuing a troubling trend, in October 2004 personal savings in the United States dropped to 0.2 percent of disposable income, according to the Commerce Department. That translates into an individual with an after-tax income of $50,000 putting about 27 cents a day into the piggy bank. That's a mere $100 a year. Incredibly, by June 2005 the savings rate slumped to zero percent.

Granted, that doesn't reflect rising residential real estate values in America or capital gains on equities, which have helped pump up the net worth of many households, especially in urban areas.

Nonetheless, even adding those additional assets doesn't sufficiently boost the total net worth of the average American family. A wide-ranging study by the Congressional Research Service (CRS) shows median net worth among all families (median meaning that half have more and half have less) to be $86,100. That includes everything: traditional household savings (bank accounts, mutual funds, and individual stocks), home equity, and retirement accounts. Fortunately, the figure is higher—$181,500—in the fifty-five to sixty-four age group nearing retirement. However, a couple hundred thousand dollars doesn't go far in a retirement that could stretch twenty to thirty years, something that's not lost on those seniors who have retired in recent years and had to return to work to make ends meet.

Most of us are unprepared for retirement. The Federal Reserve Board estimates that 37 percent of American families don't own retirement savings accounts of any kind. Among those who do, the median value is a spare $27,000. The news is a bit better for families headed by older workers—those between the ages of fifty-five and sixty-four—but not much. In 2001, the median account value in that age group was $55,000, not nearly enough to fund even a modest retirement.

In fact, here's how the CRS described possible investment returns from those savings invested conservatively: "For a sixty-five-year-old retiring in December 2003, $55,000 would be sufficient to purchase a level, single-life annuity that would pay $408 per month, based on the federal Thrift Savings Plan's current annuity interest rate of 4.375 percent."

Only $408 a month? Even if you had paid off the mortgage and pared your expenses to the nub, that check would barely cover food, insurance, and utilities, even if you kept an eye on how often you ran the air conditioner. Adding Social Security benefits helps, but it still makes for a very lean retirement.

What about pay increases? Could they help provide the financial kick necessary for that final push into retirement? The news here isn't much better.

Pay increases have steadily headed downward in the last decade. A 2004 study by Mercer Investment Consulting showed that the gap between pay increases and inflation continues to narrow, meaning that most Americans are just about staying even. Mercer indicates that "during most of the 1990s, average pay increases hovered about two percentage points above annual inflation. (In 2004), that gap has closed to about one percentage point." A tight job market could reverse that trend. However, forecasts of pay increases over the next several years show a continuing downward drift.

The fact is that most Americans fifty years and older are unprepared financially for the retirement they so eagerly anticipate, requiring many of them to delay their entry into the golden years. Simply, we just haven't put enough money aside.

Where did all that money go? Well, throughout our prime earning years, we indulged ourselves far more than we should have. And we continue to do so.

Consumerism: We're Going to Have to Pay Off All That Stuff

Much of the world envies the American lifestyle, where bigger, better, faster, more luxurious, tastier, and less filling trump simpler, wholesome, thrifty, and less expensive.

In my part of the world, Southern California, luxury automobiles are commonplace. A beat-up, old VW camper van is likely to get more attention than a top-of-the-line Mercedes. Large tract home mini-estates—often derided as McMansions—are gobbled up by buyers even before construction is completed. Eating out regularly at restaurants is considered a birthright, even among high school students.

Granted, it's inappropriate to use Southern California's standard of living to represent the entire United States. However, I have been amazed in my travels at how American consumerism has invaded even less affluent areas of the country, as seen in satellite dishes outside ramshackle homes in rural areas, upscale farming equipment ("A six-CD player for your combine, sir?") in agricultural regions and packed restaurants wherever I've traveled. We've all been sucked into the consumer lifestyle to some extent.

Unfortunately, consumerism comes with a hefty price tag. Increasingly, Americans have been writing IOUs to fund their wants. Consumer debt has more than doubled in the past ten years, according to the Federal Reserve, due in part to historically low interest rates that have enticed even the more financially disciplined among us to buy now and pay later.

While their more fiscally conservative parents saved toward their purchases and retirement, Boomers have become adept at juggling debt. In March 2005, the Federal Reserve reported that American consumers set a new debt record of $2.12 trillion. That figure encompasses credit card debt and car and boat loans but does *not* include home mortgages. Using the most recent Census Bureau data showing 217.8 million adults in the United States, average Americans over age eighteen have saddled themselves with just under $9,800 of debt, not including what's owed on the mortgage.

Regarding that mortgage, studies show that home equity is being tapped at a furious pace to keep the good times rolling. Previous generations believed in the almost sacred goal of paying off the mortgage—or at least substantially shrinking it—to prepare for retirement. That objective has changed in recent years, as more and more families reach into the vault of home equity to fund today's dreams. In fact, a 2001 federal study (the most recent available) shows that the percentage of families headed by sixty-five to seventy-four year olds with mortgage debt has increased dramatically, jumping from about 20 percent in 1992 to over 30 percent in 2001.

Granted, many of them are reaping the rewards of rising home prices, skimming off some of their "profits." But in the process they're often starting the clock again on their mortgage, taking out thirty-year loans without considering that the mortgage will be a bigger nut in their retirement budget than it was for their parents.

Over time, we've placed ourselves in bondage, carrying financial burdens that limit our ability to retire or, more importantly, to find more fulfilling work that might pay less. We've become slaves to lifestyles that cannot be sustained unless we continue to punch the time clock. So we've locked ourselves into jobs that support our standard of living, preventing us from making career changes to satisfy our heart's desire.

Perhaps it's time to re-evaluate what constitutes "the good life."

Quality of Life: We're Going to Have to Make Sacrifices—Eventually

A cartoon in the *Wall Street Journal* shows a middle-aged man in the examining room of a doctor's office. He says to the doctor, "No, I don't take any drugs, but I do have a $30-a-day latte habit."

We would laugh, except that the cartoon hits too close to home for many of us, reflecting our addiction to everyday things that once were considered luxuries. Ninety-cent cups of coffee have morphed into $3 lattes. And even if we don't crave a daily caffeine fix, each of us has ways in which we've upgraded our lives, turning extravagances into necessities.

In two thought-provoking books, *Live Well on Less Than You Think* (New York: Times Books, 2005) and *Retire on Less Than You Think* (New York: Times Books, 2004), author Fred Brock takes aim at popular assumptions about the requirements for a comfortable life. His underlying theme is simple: Don't rely on investments for your prosperity; instead, take control of your expenses and make your money go further. That's especially helpful advice today, given the stock market of the last several years.

Brock's suggestions include: avoiding debt unless absolutely necessary; assessing the true costs of living in urban areas, especially where real estate costs and taxes have skyrocketed in the past decade; being cautious of money pits (like cars); managing major expenses (such as insurance); cutting costly habits (those lattes again); and avoiding overusing credit cards.

Americans make countless assumptions about what's required to enjoy the good life, and our expectations for a comfortable standard of living have leaped in this generation. Cars are no longer just transportation; they're ego gratification and expressions of our personalities. Vacations aren't only changes of scenery to open our horizons or provide some rest; they're opportunities to escape from jobs we can't stand and to allow ourselves to be pampered in luxury, even if it means slapping them onto the credit card to be paid off in the months or years to come. High-quality handbags or shoes simply won't do; they must come from pricier designers.

Luxuries have become necessities. We've been deceived into believing they're part of a fulfilling life. However, at some point, whether by choice or requirement, most of us will have to pare our expenses and free ourselves from this unnecessary financial bondage because it denies us the freedom to make important decisions, such as what jobs we should seek or when to retire.

Retirement: We're Going to Have to Put It Off

Retirement has become the Holy Grail of the working stiff. It is the light at the end of the tunnel for an increasing number of workers who dislike their jobs. Americans are nearing retirement age in growing numbers, and as they focus on those golden years, they're having to reset their expectations.

During the stock market boom in the late 1990s, magazines and newspapers were abuzz with stories about people in their fifties, forties, and even thirties retiring from the rat race, many of them aided by stock options or the investments they made during the dot-com bubble. We don't see many articles about thirty-year-old retirees anymore. In fact, our expectations of the age at which we can retire have been ratcheting up steadily in recent years.

Reality has set in. A 2004 survey of retirement plan participants by John Hancock Financial Services showed that the average age at which people expected to retire rose to 64.4. That was an increase of almost five years from a 1995 survey. About 18 percent of respondents said they don't expect to retire until age seventy or older, more than triple the percentage in a 1995 survey.

Undoubtedly, the stock market correction and sluggish recovery that opened the twenty-first century had an effect on people's perceptions about when they could retire. Almost 25 percent of American workers forty-five or older said they planned to postpone retirement because of poor investment results, according to a 2003 poll cosponsored by the Employee Benefit Research Institute (EBRI), a nonprofit organization in Washington, D. C.

Even those who think they're set for retirement may be deceiving themselves. Another poll by the EBRI revealed that, although about two-thirds of workers believe they'll achieve their savings objective for retirement by the time they hang up their spurs, less than half said they're actually on target to do so. About two-thirds of those surveyed said they expect to work to earn an income after "retirement," many of them simply to help make ends meet.

As mentioned earlier, most Americans simply don't have the financial resources to fund comfortable retirements. Anyone who has visited the growing number of retirement calculators sponsored by financial services companies or insurance firms has seen first-hand how quickly they'll run out of money in retirement as they draw from their nest egg over what could be twenty years or more. Even someone in his fifties who engages in a full court press to save for retirement faces a daunting challenge.

Job Satisfaction: We're Going to Have to Suck It Up or Seek More Meaningful Jobs

A 2005 report from The Conference Board, a global business leadership and research group, had disheartening news about the American worker. Its wide-ranging survey found that "only half of all Americans today say they are satisfied with their jobs, down from nearly 60 percent in 1995." And even among the 50 percent who said they were content with their jobs, only 14 percent said they were "very satisfied."

Sadly, that survey of five thousand households across the country found that 25 percent of workers said they were "just showing up to collect a paycheck."

Too many workers dread going to work.

In fact, a British medical study has shown that the most common day for a heart attack is Monday. A 2004 research paper published in the American Journal of Hypertension showed a surge in blood pressure among many in the study group as they got ready for work on Monday mornings. Granted, part of that may be due to the human body naturally building up steam for the week ahead. However, it's likely that, for some people, anxieties or depression about their jobs contribute to this spike.

Without doubt, the downward spiral in job satisfaction reflects an increasing burden placed on employees by growing demands for increased productivity and rapid technological changes. Workers are required to do more with fewer resources. I saw that firsthand during a department downsizing I was responsible for in the early 1990s when I laid off more than half my staff with little change in the scope or number of projects the group was responsible for. Those who survived the job cuts had to work even harder, which brought increasing stress and resentment.

In addition, some workers are simply bored on the job. Often, they've been doing the same thing for years. The job no longer challenges them, and they're too comfortable or too afraid to seek a different position, either at the same firm or elsewhere.

However, there seems to be something else going on: employee expectations have increased. In a poll published by the job search firm Diversified Management Resources in 2004, job seekers said that the top two things that mattered most in a new job were career advancement (34 percent) and "to earn as much money as possible" (26 percent).

Americans are taking less and less pleasure in the work of their hands and minds, increasingly working merely to move up the corporate food chain and to pay off the bills. There's never much joy in that.

However, they're stuck. Regardless of how much they dislike their jobs, they've backed themselves into a corner, working to pay off the new car, the big house, and the expensive vacation, and to put away enough money to fund retirement.

We may not like our jobs, but we're stuck in them—or so we assume.

The Bottom Line: We'll Be Working Longer at Jobs We Don't Enjoy

There's no escaping that a lot of us will face having to stay in the workforce longer than they had planned. For many, even an immediate mid-course correction of saving more and spending less will be too little too late. They'll still have to postpone retirement, remaining at jobs that are unfulfilling but that pay the bills.

Is that the only option? Buried in these assumptions is an incorrect viewpoint of the role of work in our lives. Somehow we've gotten away from the biblical model of what our jobs represent as an expression of what God has created us to do. And, not-too-surprisingly, that has less to do with paying the mortgage and more to do with living out God's purpose through our work.

Reflection Point

Key thought
There's a good chance that you, like many Americans, will be working longer than you've anticipated. That makes it all the more important for your work to provide satisfaction now and into the future.

Questions
1. Which of the storm fronts outlined in this chapter are on your radar screen?

2. Most of these "perfect storm" issues involve finances. In what ways has your lifestyle impacted your ability to seek work that might be more fulfilling?

3. If money was no object and you could pursue any job (whether fulltime employment, volunteer activity, or new responsibilities at home) or study in any field (if you're a student), what would it be? Write down the first thing that comes to mind.

4. Realistically, what would it take to prepare you for that new job, responsibility, or field of study?

5. On a scale of 1 to 10 (1 being "very fulfilling," 5 being "pretty fulfilling," and 10 being "very unfulfilling"), how would you describe the work or field of study you're now involved in? Write that number down here. _____

6. On a scale of 1 to 10 (1 being "an exact match," 5 being "a good match," and 10 being "a poor match"), how closely does your job or field of study match your innate talents, abilities, and temperament? _____

7. On a scale of 1 to 10 (1 being "not interested," 5 being "interested," and 10 being "extremely interested") how interested are you in discerning what other work or studies might be more fulfilling? _____

8. Add up the numbers from the previous three questions. _____ If they total 15 or less, perhaps you're already engaged in work or studies that tap your core God-given talents. If they total 16 or more, it's possible that God may be calling you to do something different.

CHAPTER TWO

The Real
Purpose of Work

While they were worshiping the Lord and fasting,

the Holy Spirit said, "Set apart for me Barnabas and Saul

for the work to which I have called them."

—*Acts 13:2*

LIKE MANY AMERICANS, I LATCHED ONTO A NUMBER OF MYTHS ABOUT WORK AT A VERY EARLY AGE. I learned a particular heresy as a sixth grader in parochial school. Sister Sebastian was explaining the story of Adam and Eve when one of my classmates raised his hand and launched the question that most of us were itching to ask: "If Adam and Eve hadn't sinned, would we have to go to school?"

Her response was as convincing as it was incorrect. No, she said, any kind of work was the result of Adam and Eve's sin against God when they ate the forbidden fruit. If they hadn't sinned, we'd still be relaxing each day in the company of God in the Garden of

Eden, without a care in the world or any work to do. No school—
and ultimately no need to go out and work.

This is an incredibly common misperception about work, that
prior to the Fall, the first humans didn't work and that God never
intended for us to labor. However, the biblical account of a purposeful life is quite different in at least seven essential ways.

1. God Does Work.

We see God busy at work from the moment the curtain rises on
Creation. In Genesis we read: "By the seventh day God had fin-
ished the *work* he had been doing. . . . And God blessed the seventh
day and made it holy, because on it he rested from all the *work* of
creating he had done" (2:2-3, emphasis added).

From Genesis through Revelation, God is intently engaged in
some form of effort. God is not a passive, arms-folded being simply
tended to by minions and content to let things happen on their
own. God is busy at work.

In his biography of Martin Luther, author Roland Bainton
wryly observes that God even "works at common occupations. God
is a tailor who makes for the deer a coat that will last for a thousand
years. He is a shoemaker who provides boots that the deer will not
outlive. . . . God is a butler who sets forth a feast for the sparrows
and spends on them annually more than the total revenue of the
king of France. Christ worked as a carpenter" (*Here I Stand: A Life
of Martin Luther*, New York: Meridian Books, 1995, p. 181).

Our God is not a God of leisure. God does stuff.

2. Since We Are Created in the Image of God, Work Is Part of Our Nature, As Well.

We read in Genesis that *God created human beings in the image of the
divine* (1:27). In other words, the image of God has been imprinted
on us and in us. It is woven into our character. Because God is a
"doer," we are made for doing as well. And that includes work.

Our deepest passions and interests can best be expressed
through what we do, whether that's through our occupation, our
role as a parent, or as a volunteer at church or in the community.

God has built into us the motivation to work. It's buried deep within our spiritual nature.

3. God Expects Us to Work for a Lifetime.

The Sabbath Commandment begins: "Six days you shall labor and do all your work . . ." (Exodus 20:9). No time limit has been placed on that. In other words, God doesn't require us to work for a certain number of years and then encourage us to retire. In fact, there's nothing about retirement as we understand the concept in America today in the Bible.

We're expected to work at something regardless of our age, income level or wealth. Jesus emphasized that, saying: "As long as it is day, we must do the work of him who sent me" (John 9:4). In other words, during the daylight of our lives, we're to be engaged in fruitful work, bringing glory to our Creator. That's the ultimate goal of our labor.

Although the work we do in serving God is important, God does invite us to rest at times, although not in the same way we understand later-life retirement. Jesus modeled rest when he routinely took time out and sought isolation from the crowds (see Matthew 14:23 and Luke 6:12). In fact, the second element of the Sabbath Commandment is ". . . but the seventh day is a Sabbath [day of rest] to the Lord your God" (Exodus 20:10), a day that is intended to provide time in the presence of God and to refresh us by giving us a break from the workweek.

Rest and relaxation are essential, but this was never the purpose for which we were created. Mirrored in the life of Jesus is the importance of doing the work that God intends.

4. God Put the First Humans to Work, Even Prior to the Fall.

This issue represents the core of our misperception about work. For those of us who grew up thinking that if the first humans had never sinned we'd all be sprawled out on our recliners with a lemonade in one hand and a TV remote in the other, it's important to realize that Adam and Eve worked in the Garden of Eden *before* the Fall occurred. We read: "The Lord God took the man and put him in the Garden of Eden *to work it and take care of it*" (Genesis 2:15, emphasis added).

Adam, later joined by Eve, tended the garden God had created. But the nature of that work changed after they disobeyed God by eating the forbidden fruit. What had previously been easier and more enjoyable work became arduous once sin entered the picture. God tells Adam after he sinned, "Cursed is the ground because of you; through painful toil you will eat of it all the days of your life" (Genesis 3:17).

The sin of those first humans still curses us today by making work more difficult than it otherwise would have been. In spite of that, however, we're still expected to get out there and work.

5. We Are Coworkers with God.

Our work is to be done in partnership with our Lord. That was certainly the case with Adam and Eve. God created the Garden, and they were its caretakers. As God's created ones, we share their initial assignment. God has chosen to use human beings to make a difference in this world. And making a difference requires some elbow grease.

We recall in Scripture others who partnered with God to do the work that needed to be done:

- God's plans for saving at least a small portion of humanity would have been thwarted without Noah throwing his muscle into building the ark.
- The Hebrews' successful entry into God's Promised Land would not have taken place without the leadership of Moses.
- Jesus' mission to spread the gospel would have been stunted without the dedication of the disciples.
- God's plan to bring salvation to the Gentiles would have been delayed without the unwavering commitment of a former Jewish leader named Paul to carry the message to the far reaches of the ancient world.

With regard to the work of God's kingdom, there's a symbiotic relationship between God and each of us. Our work will not be successful without God's blessing, and, conversely, God's plans are hindered without our willingness to do the work.

6. Our Work Is Intended to Glorify God.

Many of us see work as "the daily grind," kind of a necessary evil. That view, however, is inconsistent with Scripture and with Christian teaching over most of the last two thousand years. Even in its earliest days, Christianity had a viewpoint of work that was markedly different than that of the surrounding culture.

In his Labor Day 2005 BreakPoint radio broadcast, Prison Fellowship Ministry founder Chuck Colson reminded listeners that "in the ancient world, the Greeks and Romans looked upon manual work as a curse, something for the lower classes and slaves. But Christianity changed all of that. Christians viewed work as a high calling—a calling to be coworkers with God in unfolding the rich potential of his creation."

The craftsman guild movement of the Middle Ages, a predecessor of modern labor unions, also had its beginnings in the church. The guilds not only set new standards of good workmanship, they also promoted the concept that there was a higher calling to the work being done by European craftsmen.

During the Reformation, Martin Luther advocated that all work should be done to glorify God and that all honest work was pleasing to him. This was the precedent for what's still called the Protestant work ethic.

However, American culture has reverted back to a more secular view of work. Colson notes: "Much of [today's] culture has a distinctly Greek view of work: We work out of necessity. But, you see, we are made in the image of God, and as such we are made to work—to create, to shape, to bring order out of disorder."

In correcting the modern American mindset, God whispers "So whether you eat or drink or whatever you do, do it all for the glory of God" (1 Corinthians 10:31).

7. We Have Been Given Specific Skills and Talents to Do the Work God Intends.

Among my greatest revelations in daily devotion and prayer time were two verses in the book of Jeremiah. The first is found in the opening, in which God tells the prophet, "Before I formed you in the womb I knew you, before you were born I set you apart" (1:5). Seventeen chapters later, God reaches across the centuries to tell us, "Like clay in the hand of the potter, so you are in my hand" (18:6b).

God has built into each of us a unique combination of skills and talents, which God then weaves into an incredible tapestry of abilities necessary for the world to function and for life to continue. God's person-specific handiwork ensures that all of us don't grow up to become doctors or police officers or stay-at-home parents or plumbers or astronomers.

The logic of that became clear to me in high school. I used to marvel at students in my chemistry class who grasped the details of atoms and molecular structure, concepts I struggled with, even after repeating chemistry because I flunked it the first time. How were they able to understand those principles that I knew I would never comprehend, no matter how much I studied or how many hours I spent with a tutor? The answer came in my English class, where some of those same science whizzes struggled with diagramming sentences or writing essays, which I excelled at.

It's all about how God hardwires us. As with Jeremiah, God has created us with specific gifts that are best used in specific areas of endeavor. What I've been called to do is likely different than what you were created for. And the same God who "made me in the womb" (Job 31:15) continues to try to mold the clay of each of us into someone unique with a specific purpose.

In that context, work is far more than something that pays the bills and keeps us occupied. It's a joint venture between God and us, in which God supplies us with specific, unique talents and abilities and invites us to serve him and his greater purposes.

Certainly, that's what God had in mind for the prophet Jonah. However, Jonah had other plans.

Reflection Point

Key thought

The importance of your work transcends merely allowing you to earn a living. It's one of the most important ways in which you can live out God's purpose. Ultimately our work can be an expression of what we were created by God to do.

Questions

1. Specifically, how do you see evidence of God busy at work? In creation? In music and art? In what's happening in the world? In your life and others around you?

2. What, if anything may be wrong with the traditional model of American retirement (stop working and pursue typical retirement activities like travel, golf, and hobbies)?

3. How do you see work as being part of our spiritual nature?

4. What does it mean to be a coworker with God? Why does God seek our help?

5. What is your life's work ultimately intended to do? Does the work you're currently doing—or intend to do—glorify God in some way? If not, how might you change your approach to the work?

Part Two

· · · · · · · · · · · · · · ·

Jonah
at the Workplace

Heaven is blessed with perfect rest,

but the blessing of earth is toil.

—*Henry Van Dyke*

By working eight hours a day

you may eventually get to be a boss

and work twelve hours a day.

—*Robert Frost*

CHAPTER THREE

Meet Jonah

The word of the LORD came to Jonah son of Amittai:

"Go to the great city of Nineveh and preach against it,

because its wickedness has come up before me."

—*Jonah 1:1*

Jonah proved that you can't keep a good man down.

—*Anonymous*

POPULAR CULTURE HAS REDUCED JONAH TO A CARICATURE. In countless cartoons and paintings, he's simply a hapless, little man pushed off a gangplank, swallowed by a whale, and then coughed up on land. However, there's far more to the story of this eighth century B.C. prophet, as we'll see later. He was chosen by God for a tough assignment: going into enemy territory that was inhabited by the fearsome Assyrians. It was a risky mission, one that Jonah initially resisted as he fled in the opposite direction, ironically putting himself and others in even greater peril than if he would have heeded God's call.

Jonah is clearly a man for the ages. His story echoes the modern dilemma we face in our own quest to hear God's voice and live according to God's call. The story of Jonah has also been the subject of debate among Bible scholars. Many argue that the story is like a parable that shows God's love and compassion in reaching out to an evil nation and how God requires his followers to bring the message of salvation to all people.

Today, as our nation finds itself in a continuing struggle with terrorists, some of whom live in modern-day Assyria (Iraq), that message seems to hit all too close to home. How do we love enemies who kill innocent people in tall buildings, in trains, and on busses? It's not easy to go to those who wish our destruction and work for peace, but that is exactly what Jonah was called to do.

Other students of the Bible declare that Jonah's story is very real, and that it is not only possible, but probable, that the events of the story happened just as Scripture describes. They use Jesus' reference to Jonah in Matthew 12:40, archaeological evidence and even some remarkable stories of human survival to declare that Jonah really was swallowed by a "large fish" (not a whale, as the popular myth has repeated) and survived to carry out God's plan to bring the Ninevites to their knees in repentance.

Regardless of how you view the literal nature of the Jonah account, his short story is remarkably full of truth. It still speaks to us in the twenty-first century. When we persistently try to live outside of God's will or reject our true calling in life, we can become adrift, or tossed about as in a storm. In spite of being blessed with enormous material blessings, many Americans experience growing frustration. That frustration is especially evident in our attitudes toward our jobs. And, for the most part, our dissatisfaction with work often results from not living out the purposes for which God created us. We've tried to be master and commander of our life, but we follow a course that often has little to do with the plans that God has for us, or which does not tap into the gifts and talents God has given us "from our mother's womb."

That was true for Jonah. God called him to a bold and remarkable ministry, bringing the word of God to the lost people of Nineveh. The story does hint that Jonah ran not just because he feared facing his enemies. He ran precisely because he knew God was a loving God who would forgive the Ninevites, his country's feared enemies (see Jonah 4:2). Jonah focused on his own needs and set his own course away from the place God called him to go. His flight was not just away from Nineveh but also away from God. He simply could not accept God's call.

Discerning God's call in our lives is not easy. It requires listening to God's spirit with our inner voice and listening to the wisdom and experience of others. Let's turn to Jonah's experience first to see what we can learn.

As we take the Jonah story apart piece by piece, let's try to connect it to our own experience.

1. God Speaks.

"The word of the LORD came to Jonah, son of Amittai" (Jonah 1:1). God is quoted directly in both the opening and closing chapters of the Bible, and God speaks throughout human history. God talked to Abraham, Moses, Jeremiah, Matthew, Mary, Paul, and countless others. God continues to speak to us today, especially through the pages of Scripture, which are *"God-breathed"* (2 Timothy 3:16). In addition, God speaks directly to our minds and our hearts (see Jeremiah 31:33). Despite popular perception, God still speaks to his people. It's just that the loud hum of our lives often drowns out God's voice. We've stopped listening. As a result, like Jonah, we often avoid moving in the direction God is leading us.

2. God Has New Plans for Jonah.

"Go to the great city of Nineveh and preach against it, because its wickedness has come up before me" (1:2). God urges Jonah to preach to the people of Nineveh, the ancient city whose ruins lie across the Tigris River from the modern-day Mosul, Iraq. It's easy to understand why Jonah was so reluctant to go to Nineveh. As Assyria's capital, it was a large city with more than 120,000 residents, surrounded by a wall almost eight miles long and 150 feet tall in places. The Assyrians were renowned in the ancient world for their savagery. They presented a real and present danger to Israel's northern kingdom at the time of Jonah. Not merely content to conquer their enemies, the Assyrians were skilled in torture. One technique called for peeling the skin off prisoners, literally skinning them alive. Ancient reliefs also show prisoners impaled upon stakes outside the city walls of a Judean city the Assyrians had conquered. The book of Nahum calls Nineveh "the city of blood" in which there are "bodies without number, people stumbling over corpses" (Nahum 3:1, 3).

God calls us all to lives of service. Depending on our gifts and abilities, the call can be simple or grand. For Jonah, the call was huge. Where do we get the resources to hear and follow? Jonah seemed to be on his own, but we have resources at our disposal. We will discuss this more later.

One of the things God should provide for us sometimes is a seat belt. A life lived as a disciple of Christ is often a full throttle experience with more twists and turns than a mountain road. If we're willing to commit our lives to God's purposes, the ride is almost sure to be exciting and sometimes bumpy! And, from time to time, God may choose to change our direction on a moment's notice.

3. Jonah Resists.

"But Jonah ran away from the LORD and headed for Tarshish" (1:3a). Jonah initially resists God's call. In fact, he flees, boarding a ship headed for Tarshish, a city farther away and literally at the opposite end of the ancient world from Nineveh. Joppa, the port

city from which Jonah departs, is six hundred miles from Nineveh, comparable to a drive across Texas. However, Tarshish, his escape destination, is a grueling three thousand miles by sea, farther than sailing from Los Angeles to Hawaii. Clearly, Jonah goes to great lengths to avoid God's assignment.

The adventures into which God leads us are sometimes scary. They take us out of our comfort zone. They involve risk, sometimes considerable. We are asked to leap from cliffs. Jonah's call was like that. That's partly why Jonah packs his bags and heads in the opposite direction when he gets the call from God. We laugh at Jonah for thinking he can elude God, yet we often do the same thing. Perhaps it's because the direction in which God is trying to lead us often seems impractical or inconsequential to *our* goals. Why spend time each day in prayer, worship, and Scripture reading when we're already so pressed for time? Why allow him to throw a monkey wrench into our carefully crafted plans when we've already put so much into our careers? Why take risks that might raise the eyebrows of family, friends, and coworkers? As with Jonah, it has to do with obedience. In 2 Corinthians 10:5, Paul reminds us to "demolish arguments and every pretension that sets itself up against the knowledge of God and . . . take captive every thought to make it obedient to Christ." God continues to call us to risky new ventures. And we resist that invitation at our own peril.

4. God Intervenes.

"Then the Lord sent a great wind on the sea, and such a violent storm arose that the ship threatened to break up" (1:4). One of the greatest mysteries in the corporate world is why a successful leader doesn't usually stay at the top of his game forever. Often, even the smartest and most committed CEOs make mistakes or lose their momentum, bringing down themselves and sometimes their companies. Why is that? Simply put, nothing lasts forever. For all of us, there comes a time to move on, no matter how successful we are in our work. In similar ways, God often intervenes in our lives to drive home the point that it's time to move on to something else. We see it when we find ourselves frustrated in our work and no longer

sense the blessing that once covered us in our endeavors. God still intervenes, but it's usually in a more subtle way than what Jonah experienced. And things start to go wrong when we're not open to God's change of plans.

5. Others Are Affected.

"So they asked [Jonah], 'Tell us, who is responsible for making all this trouble for us?'" (1:8). We're not the only ones affected when we live outside of or try to run away from God's call. Often, our families and others close to us bear the brunt. However, it can also ripple outward from there, affecting bosses, subordinates, peers, members of our church, and others who depend on us. The effects of following our own course and not God's don't remain localized. Like the rings radiating from a rock thrown in a pond, the waves generated by our avoidance of God lap up against shores more distant than we ever imagined. In the process, our behavior negatively affects others. How much depression, alcoholism, marital infidelity, and gambling addiction is due to individuals trying to fill a hole or drown a disappointment that could have been resolved by embracing the career or activity that God was trying to lead him or her toward?

6. Others Try to Help.

"Instead, the men did their best to row back to land" (1:13). Others notice when we're evading God's true calling in our lives. They may not understand exactly what's happening to us or why we've changed. But they know something is wrong, and they often try to assist. Loved ones will notice a sadness or depression and try to provide additional support. Others might make excuses for our behavior. Still others might try to cover for us, hoping our superiors won't notice our dip in performance. In the process, we drag others—often those who we love most—down into the depths with us.

7. God Grabs Jonah's Attention.

"But the LORD provided a great fish to swallow Jonah" (1:17a). The timeworn saying "You can run, but you can't hide" has some

application here as God persists in trying to bring our lives into harmony with God's calling and our true purpose. Many of us assume that if we ignore God or put him off long enough, God will finally move on. In doing so, we mistakenly underestimate God's caring determination. God can outlast even the most reluctant among us. As if God speaking to him from a burning bush wasn't enough to grab his attention, Moses tried to shield his life from God's plans by complaining that he was ill-equipped to go toe-to-toe with Pharaoh ("I don't speak well in public. Plus, why would Pharaoh even listen to a nobody like me?"). Yet, God persisted in making Moses the leader of one of the greatest liberations ever recorded. I used to believe that God works on us for a while but finally gives up and moves on to someone else if we don't concede. I learned firsthand that I was wrong about that. God never gives up on us.

8. Jonah Is Isolated.

"*. . . and Jonah was inside the fish three days and three nights*" *(1:17b)*. The crew finally heaves Jonah into the sea. Immediately, the wind and waves are calmed. And as Jonah treads water alongside the ship, God brings up "a great fish" that swallows Jonah. He remains trapped in the belly of the monstrous fish for three days and three nights. Cocooned inside the beast, Jonah has a change of heart. He begins praying and singing praises to God. He thanks God for delivering him from drowning, pays tribute to God for his incredible power, and has an epiphany in which he finally commits himself to doing what God has asked.

People who suffer from depression or living a life that is out of tune with one's core values sometimes describe feeling like they're stuck in a deep, dark hole from which they can't escape. That must have been how Jonah felt. When we're trying to escape from God we become more and more isolated. The Lord can seem more remote even to those of us who have enjoyed an intimate, vibrant relationship with him. This can be caused by our unwillingness to take bigger steps in faith that would deepen our relationship with God. It's not that God has purposefully moved farther away from us; it's that our determination to follow our own course has veered us in a different direction than the one God is headed in. What was previously a side-by-side relationship slowly becomes more and more distant. That widening gap is what makes us feel so isolated—from God and from others.

9. Jonah Reflects.

"From the depths of the grave I called for help, and you listened to my cry" (2:1b). Isolation often brings reflection. When we are disconnected from God, we're forced to consider what caused the wheels to come off the wagon of life. Human nature often encourages us to turn away from God and rely on ourselves when times are good only to return to God again when storm clouds gather. As a nation we spent time reflecting and searching for answers following the September 11th terrorist attacks on the East Coast. The horror of that day drove many marginally involved Christians back to their churches, where Sunday worship services were suddenly packed to the rafters. That only lasted for a while. My church saw a 20 percent increase in worship attendance in the weeks following the terrorist attacks, only to have it go back to pre-9/11 days a few months later. It's easier to be self-sufficient when things are going well. But we're much more reflective and open to God's leading when things get tough, as they did for Jonah.

10. Jonah Changes His Mind.

"But I, with a song of thanksgiving, will sacrifice to you. What I have vowed I will make good" (2:9). Most of us guard our life's plans jealously. We've planned out our future, many of us developing ambitions as early as college about what life should be like and what professions we would pursue. As we progress through life, we can become even more obstinate, avoiding at all costs any changes to the plan.

Predictably, we work hard to make our mark in the early years of our careers. As we hit the midpoint, we make an even greater push to achieve our hopes and dreams for success and to enhance our reputations. Then, as we turn the corner and begin considering retirement, we do everything possible to ensure that we'll have sufficient financial resources to carry us through our later years. We don't want to rock the boat. We avoid doing anything along the way that threatens our plans and assumptions. However, there come times, some of them God ordained, when we must change the game plan because it's not supposed to work out as we'd hoped. We're confronted with something so compelling—and so obvious, in retrospect—that to stay on the same course becomes increasingly risky, even more perilous than allowing our plans to be changed.

11. Jonah Does What He's Supposed To.

"Jonah obeyed the word of the LORD and went to Nineveh" (2:3a). You can almost sense the relief in Jonah once he commits to following God's lead. It's the same with us when we decide to do the right thing. Gradually, we're brought back in step with God, and we again feel closeness to God. Once we make that decision, God blesses us with the peace that has been so elusive.

12. Jonah Succeeds.

"When God saw what they did and how they turned from their evil ways, he had compassion and did not bring upon them the destruction he had threatened" (3:10). Success is assured when we follow God. One caution, however: It may not be the type of success we had envisioned or, in Jonah's case, the success he even desired. As we said earlier, Jonah didn't exactly like the idea of God forgiving the Ninevites. He even sulks a bit, when his message results in the Ninevites repenting (4:9-10). Their evil and debauchery went far beyond what he hoped God would forgive. In spite of Jonah's reluctance, God blessed Jonah's efforts in a remarkable way with an incredible outcome. So it is when we finally give in and do what God has called us to do.

Reflection Point

Key thought

> *The account of Jonah is far more than a simple fish story. Within its pages is an example of what happens when God's plan collides with human will and the unfortunate fallout that results from not heeding God's call. Jonah clearly heard God's call. Yet he chose to flee, hoping to outrun or outlast the God who was urging Jonah to do something very different with his life. God still does that today, and our response is often similar to Jonah's.*

Questions

1. God challenged Jonah to a difficult task. Jonah was being asked to do something that was not just inconvenient or uncomfortable, but he could be killed in carrying it out. How does our culture turn us into Jonahs, encouraging us to look out more for our own interests than for God's interests?

2. What are the obstacles that prevent you from hearing God's voice or at least sensing God's direction?

3. How do we affect others when we become like Jonah, attempting to run away from the course that God is setting for us? How has your dissatisfaction with your job or possible career choice rubbed off on others, perhaps family members, friends, or those you work with? Have they noticed your dissatisfaction in your work?

4. What would it take to reassure you that God will help things work out if you pursued other opportunities in your work or studies?

5. How willing are you to trust God in at least a few baby steps of faith toward realizing the purpose for which God may be calling you?

6. What are your core values? Name at least five. How are those values in tune with God and God's calling in your life?

Part Three

· · · · · · · · · · · · · ·

The Quest
for Significance

Don't forget until too late that the business of life

is not business but living.

—*B. C. Forbes*

Don't let the good things of life rob you of the best things.

—*Maltbie D. Babcock*

The best things in life . . . aren't things.

—*Anonymous*

CHAPTER FOUR

Desperation in the Midst of Abundance

Then Jesus said to his disciples, "I tell you the truth,

it is hard for a rich man to enter the kingdom of heaven."

—Matthew 19:23

JONAH LIVED IN A BRIEF PERIOD OF PROSPERITY FOR ISRAEL. Under King Jeroboam II, the empire was expanding. Its capital, Samaria, was being refortified with double walls to repel invaders, all to protect the kingdom's increasing prosperity.

However, Israel's attention was diverted from the God whose blessings made all of this possible. Under Jeroboam the kingdom increasingly engaged in oppression, idolatry, wastefulness, and drunkenness. God's people were blinded by their apparent safety, security, and wealth. Times were pretty good, so they turned away from God. And, as was often the case, they were unfulfilled by all of their blessings.

There's certainly a parallel between Israel in the eighth century B.C. and our own modern experience. We enjoy prosperity today undreamed of by even our grandparents. In fact, by almost any measure, we are surrounded by greater abundance than anyone in the history of humankind.

We live longer and healthier lives, eat greater varieties of foods, enjoy larger living spaces, luxuriate ourselves with more comforts, and live with greater physical security than anyone who has walked the earth before us.

Most of us assume we'll never have to be hungry. We have access to twenty-four-hour entertainment, grocery superstores, year-round climate control, personal transportation, and middle-class homes that would qualify as mansions in most of the world.

We have more stuff and less joy, the result of creeping consumerism, a trend that John Kavanaugh, in his book *Following Christ in a Consumer Society*, defined as "a system of reality (a philosophy of what is most real and valuable) and a religion (a belief that saves us and gives us ultimate meaning)" (Maryknoll, New York: Orbis Books, 1991). One of the big problems in our modern consumer society is that we define ourselves according to what we "have" rather than by who we are. A popular bumper sticker sums it up as simply: "I shop; therefore I am."

America's material prosperity is truly incredible. A few examples:

- Until recently, the fastest growing segment of single-family home real estate was second homes or vacation homes. In 2004, they made up one out of every three houses sold in the United States.
- Homes with air conditioning are now standard. In fact, even homes in northern or coastal regions that rarely have heat spikes often have central air conditioning, a former luxury that has become an expectation.
- Americans continue to accumulate more and more stuff, contributing to the explosive growth in self-storage facilities. Almost forty thousand of them are scattered across the country, according

to the Self Storage Association. That's up from only twenty-two thousand a little more than a decade ago. This is in spite of the fact that the average house has grown by more than 50 percent in the last three decades, from about 1,500 square feet to 2,300 square feet.

- Approximately 750,000 all-terrain vehicles are sold in the United States every year. Most of these ATVs, many costing $5,000 or more, are used exclusively for recreation.
- Especially curious is the growth of "fly-through" restaurants located in small airports. Many of them are found in remote areas accessible only by airplane. Somebody's got to feed all those hungry private pilots in the mood for a slab of ribs.

What's interesting is the effect our increased prosperity has had on average Americans. This tectonic shift in prosperity hasn't just affected the rich or ruling classes, as has happened historically. Largely, it has benefited the middle class. Many who frequent those fly-through restaurants are middle-class people enjoying their growing disposable income.

Yet, we are increasingly unhappy. In *The Progress Paradox* (New York: Random House, 2003), author Gregg Easterbrook cites a Yale University study showing that, compared to 1950, ten times as many people in the United States and Western Europe today report suffering from general depression without a specific cause.

Despite our ability to fly into an airport to grab a hamburger, there's something missing. We've lost our way. Deep within us, we sense that we're not on the right path. No matter how many job promotions we earn, how much wealth we acquire, or how much comfort we sink into, we still feel unfulfilled and unhappy in our jobs. We have never found the joy that all this "stuff" promised to deliver. Like the Israel of Jonah's time, we have forgotten the source of our abundance and have allowed the pursuit of wealth—or at least "security"—to increasingly override our ability to hear God's calling. We seek to take care of our own needs, and we've stopped asking what God wants us to do.

Is this really the way it's supposed to be?

Deep within us we groan with questions for which there are no simple answers: "Is there more to life than a paycheck? Am I really doing what I'm supposed to do during my lifetime? Why isn't my job more fulfilling?

The Quest for Meaning

Many workers in the first two centuries of our nation's history were focused on conquering something. Often that meant surmounting the challenges of the American wilderness, the raw land and resources that harbored so much potential. Great vision and effort went into taming that wilderness, turning woodlands and meadows into farmland, making rivers navigable and transforming wagon paths into roadways. That involved monumental effort and vision.

Unfortunately, today many of us are lost in the workplace wilderness searching for significance. Except for a few cutting-edge companies that are blazing new trails in the products and services they provide, employees at most firms are simply tinkering with products and formulas that have been fairly successful. They're not taming new frontiers. It's far more difficult to develop a passion for work in this environment. Mired in routine paperwork, spreadsheets, and e-mail, there's little vision or excitement in what many of us do day to day.

Even those who have achieved success in their work often haven't found much significance. They're often either bored or frustrated in what they do. They feel stymied. Any creativity they once itched to express has long since drained away on the job.

That point was driven home at a retirement celebration I attended recently. During a video tribute to the retiree, one of her coworkers remarked that her retirement "will result in the blossoming of her creativity." You mean to tell me that she's been keeping all that creativity pent up inside of her while on the job for the past twenty-five years?

Unfortunately, it's what could be said about many of us in the workforce. It's why we look for "creative outlets" outside of work, often in the form of hobbies or volunteer activities.

Part of the reason why many of us do not find meaning in our jobs is because we really don't care about the work we do. We're part of the working wounded who show up because it's the only way we know how to put food on the table and keep gas in the car. Even if our success affords us a more affluent lifestyle, we're still left searching for deeper meaning in what we do.

That issue is addressed in a growing number of books, the topics of which are best captured in the title *From Success to Significance* (New York: Zondervan, 2004), a thoughtful book by Lloyd Reeb. Even those of us who have accomplished a lot still yearn for the significance that only comes from doing what God has uniquely created us to do. And we'll continue to struggle with the meaning of life until we determine God's calling and the true purpose of our work.

Reflection Point

Key thought

> Many of our lives today epitomize what Marie von Ebner-Eschenbach wrote about in the nineteenth century: "To be satisfied with little is hard; to be satisfied with a lot, impossible." Although blessed with great prosperity, a growing number of us feel unfulfilled. In our focus on abundance we've shifted our sights off what God intends for our lives. Perhaps you, too, are feeling more successful than significant.

Questions

1. Do you consider your life "successful," "significant," or both?

2. List those aspects of your life that have made you successful and those that have given your life significance.

Measures of my life's successes	Measures of my life's significance

3. How can you combine aspects of your responses in the two columns above in whatever work you do or in studies you are pursuing?

4. In what way could your life be used by God in a more significant way? In what way could your life better glorify God and better utilize the talents and skills God has given you?

CHAPTER FIVE

Discovering God's Purpose in Our Work

"I just can't help feeling they got him so screwed up running

in a circle that he's forgotten what he was born to do."

—*Horse trainer Tom Smith in the movie* Seabiscuit

IT'S NO ACCIDENT THAT RICK WARREN'S BOOK *THE PURPOSE-DRIVEN LIFE®* HAS SOLD MORE THAN TWENTY-FIVE MILLION COPIES. In it he helps readers answer the age-old question, "What on Earth am I here for?" The book's opening chapter clearly outlines the paradigm shift we have to make to find the answers to life's most vexing questions. Pastor Warren writes:

> The search for the purpose of life has puzzled people for thousands of years. That's because we typically begin at the wrong starting point—ourselves. We ask self-centered questions like

What do *I* want to be? What should I do with *my* life? What are *my* goals, *my* ambitions, and *my* dreams for *my* future? But focusing on ourselves will never reveal our life's purpose." (*The Purpose-Driven Life®: What on Earth Am I Here For?* Grand Rapids, Mich.: Zondervan, 2002, p. 17)

In childhood, we were taught to put ourselves first whenever someone asked us, "So, what do *you* want to be when you grow up?" No one ever asked us, "What does *God* want you to be when you grow up?" In the absence of that provocative query, we've been trained to think that what we do with our lives completely revolves around us and our own ambitions.

Most high school counseling programs, college admission applications, and career counselors foster that me-centrism. The waters get muddied further when we enter the workforce and do work that carries out what we've been trained for, again simply tapping into our self-centered hopes and dreams. Along the way, things get further garbled as ambition, ego, greed, and fear enter the picture, all human frailties that take us further and further away from God's promise, as stated in Jeremiah 29:11, "For I know the plans I have for you . . . plans to prosper you and not to harm you, plans to give you hope and a future."

A 2005 survey by The Barna Group shows that, while Christians say their priorities have shifted in recent years, being more discerning about God's purpose in their work life hasn't been part of that change. Instead, life priorities have shifted toward having a more satisfying family life (#1), living out the principles of faith (#2), and having good friends (#3). That's unfortunate because finding fulfillment in our work can ultimately result in greater joy in all three of those areas.

If we are the clay that God wants to mold, shouldn't we allow ourselves to be fashioned into performing the job that God has in mind for us, one which taps our specific talents, abilities, and passions? Now, you may indeed be doing the work God has called you to do. That's great. Keep it up. But, if you are like I was, you are not in work that is satisfying; you aren't experiencing a greater connection to God's true calling for you.

Lisa's Story

Let's look at Lisa, a recent college graduate. She and her family have been close friends of ours for many years, and we've known her since she was about two years old. Lisa is a born teacher. That was clear at a very early age as she continually herded together the other kids in the neighborhood to play school. She was always the teacher, setting up classrooms in our house and hers. Her students loved her and their time in her classroom. She had a natural gift for teaching and she made class time fun. She developed sophisticated activities and lesson plans, even though she was no older than some of the nine- and ten-year-olds she taught.

Although teaching continued to be in her heart, Lisa resisted the call. In fact, when she went off to college she decided to major in communications. Four years later, she received her degree and went off to work in the field of corporate communications. She struggled in finding the right job, trying several corporate and agency positions and finding them unfulfilling.

Eventually, she returned to school, this time to earn—you guessed it—a teaching credential. When I saw her recently, she radiated enthusiasm in her decision to go back to school and to pursue the career for which clearly she was built. Lisa is more fortunate than most, having learned earlier in life than most to follow the passion that God breathed into her.

Each of us was born for a reason and for a purpose. That God-given purpose can be fulfilled through our work, whether as a business owner, employee, craftsman, stay-at-home parent, or full-time volunteer.

God has a purpose for you in your work. As soon as you discover it and start living it, you'll find fulfillment and joy beyond what you can ever imagine. However, to experience that, you must stop pursuing merely what *you* want and start doing what God created you to do.

The Concept of *"Vocare"*

Vocare (vo-CAR-eh) is Latin for "the call." It describes the specific call to vocation that God places in our minds and in our hearts. Unfortunately, it's a term that has been terribly underrated over the centuries. In the Middle Ages, the church held that only certain people were "called" to serve God, those who held positions in the church, such as priests and nuns.

Martin Luther railed against such a narrow definition, arguing that everyone receives a specific call from God. He believed that the concept of *vocare* was applicable in three specific areas of society, what he called the "ecclesiastical" (matters of the church), the "political" (the governing, educating, and protecting of people and enforcing of laws), and the "domestic" (pretty much everything else, including commerce and family life). Luther argued that God calls all people to what he refered to as the "priesthood of all believers." By virtue of baptism, we are all called to serve as God's "ministers" in the world.

The misperception of who gets "the call" continues today. Many of us assume that God specifically calls only the clergy. The rest of us can do whatever we want.

Nothing could be further from the truth. What each of us does is of great interest to God. Frederick Buechner, in his book of daily meditations called *Listening to Your Life* (San Francisco: Harper-Collins, 1992), observes, "We can speak of choosing our vocation, but perhaps it is at least as accurate to speak of a vocation's choosing us, of a call's being given and our hearing it or not hearing it."

Why wouldn't our vocations be of interest to God? Of the 1,440 minutes each of us is given every day, the greatest block of time is usually spent on the work we do. God is keenly interested in how we spend our time, including work.

A person's *vocare* can change over time, as we'll see in the next chapter. In God's "economy" our vocation or calling has the following purposes:

- To provide a way to express our love for God (see Colossians 3:23-24);
- To be a witness to others (1 Thessalonians 4:9-12);

- To serve others, using the skills and talents God has blessed us with (Matthew 25:14-30);
- To provide us with a ministry (2 Corinthians 5:20);
- To meet the financial needs of ourselves and our families (1 Timothy 5:8);
- And to earn income to help the less fortunate and spread the Gospel (Ephesians 4:28-29).

How do we fulfill these ambitious purposes in our chosen work? That question lies at the heart of discovering our deepest vocational calling.

Reflection Point

Key thought

The Bible answers one of humankind's must enduring questions: "Why am I here?" Scripture reveals that we were created to glorify God and to be God's partners, extending his reach into the workplace, home, and school. God calls us to discover our own vocare.

Questions

1. Among the six-and-a-half-billion people in the world today, why do you think God specifically created you?

2. What specific, and perhaps unique, talents has God given you that can be utilized in the work you do?

3. Are you able to utilize those skills in the work you are currently doing? If not, are you aware of a job, course of study, or volunteer activity in which you could more effectively use your God-given talents and skills?

4. Does your current *vocare* serve any or all of the following biblical purposes?
   - ❑ Provides a way to express your love for God
   - ❑ Uses the skills and talents God has blessed you with
   - ❑ Provides you with a "ministry" of some sort
   - ❑ Serves others in a meaningful way
   - ❑ Meets the financial needs of you and your family
   - ❑ Allows you to earn an income to help those less fortunate and to spread the gospel

5. If your current job or field of study doesn't allow you to answer "yes" to any of the boxes above, what job or vocation would better allow you to do that?

6. If you answered "yes" to everything in question 4 but still are struggling in your work, why is this so?

7. What changes would you need to make to your life and/or lifestyle to allow you to embrace the vocation God intends for you?

Part Four

· · · · · · · · · · · · · · · ·

The Jonah Factor

God is not of common sense but of revelation.

—*Oswald Chambers*

The purpose of life is this:

Love God and do what you want.

—*St. Augustine*

CHAPTER SIX

What Is
The Jonah Factor?

We have done so not according to worldly wisdom

but according to God's grace.

—2 Corinthians 1:12

WE GET THE SENSE THAT THINGS WERE GOING WELL FOR JONAH UNTIL GOD CHANGED THE PLAN. Up to that point, Jonah was likely engaged in activities similar to most other Old Testament prophets. He was Yahweh's conscience for and mouthpiece to God's people, reminding them of what they should and should not do. He may have foretold events to come and warned them about sinful ideologies and practices that would separate them from God. He probably planned to continue in that ministry until he died. However, things went south—or, literally, west—when God issued new orders, pointing Jonah in a different direction and out of his comfort zone. Jonah resisted, and at that point a gulf developed between Jonah and his God.

It's not unusual for God to change the plans for his people. Abraham was seventy-five years old when God told him, "Leave your country, your people, and your father's household and go to the land I will show you" (Genesis 12:1). David, the future king of Israel, left lifetime employment as a shepherd to answer God's call (1 Samuel 17). Paul and other members of the first-century church were continually prodded by the Holy Spirit to change direction to fulfill their mission of spreading the gospel (Acts 16 and 18). Paul acknowledges that when he tells followers in Ephesus, "I will come back if it is God's will" (Acts 18:21).

We're rarely called to one job, or even one career, for our entire lives. Sometimes God provides one job as a stepping stone to another or as a training ground for something completely different. In some ways, it's like planting a garden, especially when putting in annuals. Over the years I've learned that even the hardiest annuals do well for only a season or two, even in temperate Southern California. The primroses I plant in the winter thrive at first in the cooler temperatures and ample rainfall. However, they start struggling in the spring and are dead by summer unless I replant them with marigolds, which are built for the heat of summer.

Likewise, we're often called to our jobs for a season or two. We have to be open to God's prompting when it's time to move on. Otherwise we wither because we're no longer planted in the right place in the right season.

Jonah learned that the hard way. Through God's direct intervention, Jonah found himself forced to realign with God and the purpose for which he had been created. Jonah had a change of heart while isolated in the belly of the great fish, the culmination of a process in which Jonah found his way back into God's presence.

It's when we're wrestling with God that we can look him in the face, as Jacob did (see Genesis 32:22-32). In the process, we not only gain a deeper understanding of God, but we also receive insights into God's direction for us.

That process provides the basis for *The Jonah Factor*.

Much like Jonah, we need a method for discerning and submitting to God's will, a process that will help to take the guesswork out of what is often a very difficult and risky decision.

God doesn't usually send a big fish to redirect us. Nowadays, God's a bit more subtle. The tools God provides are spiritual ones, which makes sense because we're told that "God is spirit" (John 4:24). When God sent the Holy Spirit at Pentecost, he introduced a new way of working in the lives of believers.

The Jonah Factor's "13 Steps" are ways for each of us to discern the Holy Spirit's leading, both now and in the future. As with Jonah, God's plans for us change over time. They're not static; God's work never is. Moses' early life, perhaps the first forty years or so, was marked by growing up and being trained in the house of Egypt's pharaoh. The following forty years he spent as a shepherd in the wilderness, and during his final forty years he served as the leader anointed to free God's people from slavery in Egypt and to lead them to the Promised Land. Like Moses, we've got to be flexible.

Simply, *The Jonah Factor* is a process by which we discern God's call and allow God to either confirm that our current life's work is what he intends for us or to lead us into the type of job, responsibility, or volunteer activity that is most in line with God's call at the time.

Before we go through those 13 Steps, perhaps you should determine whether you might be a Jonah.

Are You a Jonah?

It starts as a nagging suspicion. Over time it grows into discontent. And before you know it, you're lost. In many ways, our culture thrusts us into the role of Jonah. Social norms, customs, and cultural assumptions often cause us to default into a mindset that may be inconsistent with God's plans for us.

For example, Jonah operated with an ancient Hebrew mindset. He and the Jewish people knew they were God's "Chosen People," those with whom God had a special relationship. Many believed that this unique covenant excluded all other people. So when God commanded Jonah to travel to a pagan land to tell its barbaric warriors to repent, the order may have sounded inconsistent with Israel's belief that only they were special enough to have a close relationship with God. Sharing the word of God with the Ninevites, which would likely result in God showing them mercy, seemed inconsistent with what many of the Jews believed about God and their favored place in the world.

Jonah and his Jewish compatriots were partially right. Indeed, God had formed an exclusive bond with the people of Israel. But God never told them that this bond would be exclusive forever, that God wouldn't eventually open that door to others. That was simply their assumption, one that had become more cultural than spiritual.

What assumptions are you making that prevent you from considering and then following through on the possible plan that God has laid out for you? Is it:

- Inability to let go of your financial security blanket?
- Fear of losing income?
- Concern about loss of prestige or status within your workplace, home, church, or family?
- Unease regarding what others might say?
- Unwillingness to change your lifestyle?
- Fear of giving up something you've worked hard to achieve?

Each of us fights one or more of these assumptions when we consider doing what God shows us, especially when it involves a life change, as it did with Jonah. And, indeed, we will have to give up something to fulfill the plans that God has for us. But what glorious plans they are.

The Jonah Factor process is at odds with much of what we are taught and believe. Yet it's completely consistent with scriptural principles and how the great men and women of God throughout history discerned God's will and then followed, sometimes taking huge leaps of faith.

Warning Signs

So, what are the warning signals that indicate you might be a Jonah? They can include the following:

If you're currently employed:

- Growing dissatisfaction with your job and/or employer
- Working only to earn a paycheck
- Fear of Mondays
- Boredom at work
- Buying lottery tickets or engaging in other forms of gambling in hopes of instant wealth to afford leaving a job
- Inability to grasp or having no interest in new concepts, procedures, and technologies on the job
- Difficulty tackling new assignments

If you're a stay-at-home parent:

- Lack of fulfillment in your at-home responsibilities
- Growing disagreements with your spouse
- Increasing friction between you and your child(ren)
- Use of alcohol or medication to help cope with children, a spouse, or household responsibilities

If you're retired:

- Malaise
- Boredom
- Lack of goals and purpose
- Growing friction with your spouse
- Increased "recreational" use of alcohol or medication

If you're a college student:

- Difficulty understanding new concepts that others in class understand
- Decreasing enthusiasm in your major or area of focus
- Fear of having to leave college and go into the workplace

In your spiritual life:
- Growing distance between you and God
- Difficulty in praying or lack of interest in reading and understanding Scripture
- Lack of spiritual growth
- Inability to trust God during times of challenge
- Unwillingness to take even small steps in faith

Do any of these points hit home? If so, read on.

Modern-Day Jonahs

Early in my career I worked for a large aerospace corporation. Lots of Jonahs roamed the halls there. However, one stood head and shoulders above the others.

At that time, most aerospace firms and some other large corporations used a formula to determine when an employee could retire with full benefits. The calculation was determined by adding a person's age to his or her years of service at the company. When that totaled 85 points or more, the employee could retire with full pension and health benefits. (An example would be someone who had been with the company for thirty years and was fifty-five years old.)

These were the "golden handcuffs" that kept people at the firm longer than they wanted to be—or should have been. Unfortunately this "benefit" encouraged too many employees to become Jonahs, forsaking what God was showing them in the interest of ensuring a secure retirement.

The heartbreaking story of one Jonah at the firm is a reminder of how misguided our attempts at retirement security sometimes are.

I worked closely with Frank, a manager about two years away from his treasured 85 points. He hated his job, and it was obvious to anyone who had contact with him. Ornery and sarcastic, Frank seemed to do as little as possible during his workday, and he made life miserable for those who depended on him.

Frank had hung a big stack of Post-It Notes® on the wall next to his office door. Each of the yellow stickies had a number on it in descending order of the number of days he had left to retirement. His ritual each morning, as he walked in the door, was to tear off a yellow sticky, revealing a new number showing that he was one day closer to leaving the job he hated so much.

I asked Frank one day why he tormented himself by having to stare at those numbers all day. After all, his desk faced the doorway, which meant that his retirement countdown clock was rarely out of his sight. He explained that he liked being reminded of how many days he had left on the job because they provided a light at the end of the tunnel and gave him opportunities to dream about the fun and exciting things he would do when he finally could leave the company.

Frank did, indeed, retire on the day the countdown reached "0." His coworkers threw him a decent farewell party, complete with the gold watch that was the standard retirement gift in those days.

But that's not the end of the story.

About two months after he walked through the doorway into the life he had so long dreamed about we received a call from Frank's wife. (You can probably see this coming.) She told us that Frank had died of a heart attack. He never knew what hit him.

What a tragedy; what a wasted life.

He was a classic Jonah, but his mindset wasn't that unusual.

All too many workers in their fifties and sixties are simply hanging on, waiting for retirement. It's tragic enough when that happens to a sixty-year-old, but I've worked with many people in their forties and fifties who were in the same boat. Like Frank, some of them gutted it out at unsatisfying jobs for a long time, only to pass away shortly after grabbing the brass ring of retirement.

Even if our retirement lasts for many years, however, we've sacrificed the prime years of our lives to get there. That's equally tragic.

Over the years, I've been amazed at how many people on the summits of their careers have told me they wished they were doing something else. Most memorable is a very successful associate who dreamed of moving to New England to open a bed-and-breakfast inn. Craig and his wife had traveled there numerous times and had fallen in love with the region. He dreamed of opening a B&B that would cater to hard-working, over-stressed corporate types like himself. It would have a restaurant on the premises that served stick-to-your-ribs breakfasts and gourmet dinners.

Craig had done all the research, run the numbers, and said he had the support of his wife. He knew the 24/7 realities of running a time-consuming business like that and relished the thought of being a combination Mr. Fix-It and gourmet chef. However, he remained frozen, unable to take the next step. He simply didn't want to risk whatever financial security he thought he had. As far as I know, he never realized his dream.

Although I'm unsure of whether he had a sense of God's calling in his life, I do believe that his passion was consistent with his calling. Often, we innately sense God's calling, even though we may not know God. Craig was unsure of whether he could be successful in pursuing his dream. He wanted a guarantee. He didn't get one. So he did nothing.

Somehow, we need to realign ourselves with the plans God has for us. But how do we do that? Is there some kind of system or process that will help us discern our God-given talents and abilities, allow God to guide us in using them, and then build our confidence to move in a different direction?

This is where *The Jonah Factor* comes in.

Reflection Point

Key thought

> *It's easier to see the Jonah in others than in ourselves. Sometimes those Jonahs provide a mirror for us to examine whether we, too, are trying to escape—or put off—God's plans for us.*

Questions

1. Have you ever had the sense that it's time to move on to other work? Describe how that felt. What did you do?

2. Are you in the midst of this kind of struggle right now? What are you doing about it? What, if any, new jobs or activities have you considered?

3. Rate the importance of the following as they apply to the work you do by checking the appropriate box:

Your work provides:	Extremely important	Moderately important	Not very important
Security			
Financial success			
Early retirement			
Advancement opportunities			
Prestige/titles			
Ego gratification			
A comfortable lifestyle			
A means to pay your bills			
The ability to buy more things			

As you reflect on your priorities, are any holding you back from pursuing more meaningful, fulfilling work that God may be calling you to do?

4. Have you had even a passing thought that it might be time to change your career, course of study, or volunteer activities you're currently involved in? If so, write down, as specifically as possible, what you've been sensing?

5. Do you know someone who exemplifies Jonah? What is their demeanor like, and does he or she seem misplaced in their career, job, or whatever work they're currently doing? List the characteristics of that individual who gives you that impression.

6. Are there any similarities between you and this person in terms of what it might take to realize greater joy, especially in the work you do? What are those similarities?

CHAPTER SEVEN

13 Steps to Finding the Job of a Lifetime

But Jonah had gone below deck, where he lay down

and fell into a deep sleep.

—Jonah 1:5

MANY OF US HAVE GONE INTO A DEEP SLEEP. Our lives have become routine, perhaps comfortably so. What few plans we've made for the future mostly involve maintaining the material and financial security we mistakenly cling to. Much like Jonah, we've gone below deck, holing ourselves up against God's plans or direction, and hoping we won't get noticed.

We're following a script written by someone else, perhaps living out the expectations of our parents, our employers, our spouses, or our children. We've slipped unconsciously into lives of bondage to bosses, debts, lifestyles, and expectations in a manner captured memorably by Conrad Richter in his classic novel *The Light in the Forest*. Listen as one character in the book, a slave named Bejance, tries to show a white boy, Conrad, how subtly the yoke of bondage is applied, comparing it to how a wild horse gets broken:

> Every day they drop another fine strap around you. Little by little they buckle you up so you don't feel too much at one time. Sooner or later they have you all hitched up, but you've got so used to it by that time you hardly know it. . . . You own a house and a piece of land and pays taxes. You hoe all day in the cornfield and toil and sweat a diggin' up stumps. Piece by piece you get broke in to livin' in a stall by night, and by day pullin' burdens that mean nothin' to the soul inside of you. (New York: Bantam Books, 1953, p. 50)

None of us intended to become domesticated to the world's ways and the comforts of life. But we allowed it to happen. We were seduced into thinking that happiness comes in the form of a full stomach, a warm bed, and a tropical vacation every couple of years. All the while, more and more straps of confinement were added to our lives until many of us have ended up becoming petting zoo ponies, our waking hours spent hitched up, lumbering along in a circle.

The Jonah Factor is intended to rouse us out of the stupor we've been lulled into because life is "okay." God doesn't intend our lives to be the lukewarm day-to-day monotony many of us find ourselves in. We've been drinking from a stagnant pool instead of the fresh spring that's ours for the asking.

But how do we discover the wellhead that's out there for us? Where are those *"streams of living water"* that Jesus talks about in John 7:38? How can we get back to a place where we're excited about the adventure ahead, so much so that we anticipate getting up on Monday morning even more than the drive home from work on Friday evening?

That is the heart of *The Jonah Factor*.

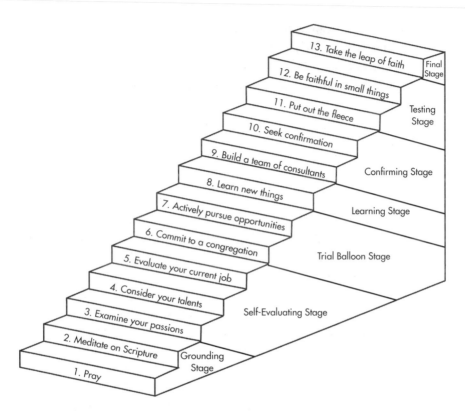

As I developed *The Jonah Factor*, it became clear to me that there were thirteen specific steps necessary to hear God's call and develop the confidence to follow it. Just as there are ten high hurdles in a 110-meter race—no more, no less—sidestepping or tripping over even one of them can prevent you from winning the race. I encourage you to take the 13 Steps in order. In addition, the steps of *The Jonah Factor* fit into seven specific stages of discernment, which I will describe later.

It's important to follow each of the stages—and the steps within them—sequentially. For example, you can't successfully move to Stage 3 until you're fully engaged in Stage 2. Hearing God's voice, synthesizing it into an action plan, testing that plan, and then moving on it is a process that requires certain things to be in place each time we take a new step.

The process is like a stairway. Each stage, and the steps within each stage, prepares you for the next one. Passing over or short-changing any of them only makes future steps and stages more difficult and increases your chances of stumbling. Much like vaulting up a stairway, skipping steps increases the odds that you'll falter.

You'll notice that the 13 Steps build to a crescendo in which you'll be asked to do something scary—take a leap of faith. Although that sounds like the most difficult step, it will be the easiest, *provided you have taken sufficient time with each step and have not skipped any.* You cannot take the leap of faith God is calling you to unless you have carefully and thoughtfully worked your way up the stairway and you are absolutely sure that what you're about to do is what God intends.

One additional caution: *The Jonah Factor* takes time. In today's over-caffeinated, get-things-done-quickly, grab-a-good-night's-sleep-in-five-hours world, we're accustomed to resolving issues and getting our questions answered very quickly. Television sitcoms and dramas may work that way, but God doesn't. As I progressed through *The Jonah Factor* process, my few missteps were the result of rushing the process along, trying to keep to my timeline instead of trusting in God's. As you go through the process, some steps may go more quickly than others, depending on where you are in your faith journey and how in tune you already are with God's will and his desires for you.

Also, you'll need to set time aside each day for this process—not easy when our waking hours are already packed with more than we can comfortably deal with. Try to find a time of day that's a bit less hectic for you and schedule some time for this. Remember, *The Jonah Factor* is intended to help you make what could be a life-changing transformation, bringing you in line—at long last—with the plans God has for you in your work.

The Jonah Factor is a journey of revelation, not a NASCAR race. Think of the process as if you were baking an apple pie. If the recipe calls for you to bake the pie at 350 degrees for forty-five minutes, turning up the heat to 450 degrees will not allow you to serve up that pie in twenty minutes. It'll ruin it. A delicious apple pie—like discerning God's will—just takes time.

With that in mind, let's get going.

Reflection Point

Key thought

> *Most of us rush through life, leaving little room each day for God to speak to us and guide us. God can't share his plan for us unless we spend time with him.*

Questions

1. What prevents you from spending more time with God in prayer, worship, and Scripture reading?
   - ❏ "My job is too demanding."
   - ❏ "I've got too much to do at school."
   - ❏ "I have too many family responsibilities."
   - ❏ "My church activities keep me running."
   - ❏ "I've been roped into volunteering for too many things."
   - ❏ "I need time to unwind in the evenings, so I watch television."
   - ❏ "My children are in sports, so I spend all my time on the soccer field."

2. Which of the responsibilities or distractions you checked in question 1 can be most easily eliminated or be made less time consuming?

3. How confident are you that God can provide a new direction for your life? Why? Are you ready to consider how God can help you discover a new sense of purpose or direction in your work?

Step 1: Pray
Listen carefully for God's "still, small voice"

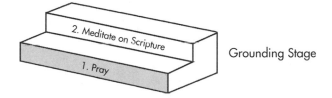

2. Meditate on Scripture

1. Pray

Grounding Stage

This first step is the most obvious, but it's also the most difficult for many of us. Amidst busy days and noisy lives we allow ourselves very few moments in quiet, peaceful reflection with God required to discern God's direction and purpose. Yet, as we are reminded in Psalm 48:10, our Lord tells us to "be still, and know that I am God." Only in those quiet periods can we hear "the still, small voice" in which God spoke to Elijah (1 Kings 19:12).

How do we discern the whisper of God's voice? And once we hear it, how can we tell if it's really God and not just our own thoughts and desires?

There are at least two requirements for hearing the voice of God. The first and most important one is making ourselves available to God. I'm continually amazed at how much time Jesus spent alone in prayer. In Matthew 14 we find Jesus at the height of his ministry. Thousands are following him. The word is out about his miracles, preaching, and wisdom. People press in from all sides, wanting his attention. "Jesus, would you heal my friend?" "Lord, can I have just a minute to ask you a question?" "Jesus, can you explain that Sermon on the Mount idea one more time?" Clearly, his days are extremely busy.

Yet in the midst of those crushing demands, Jesus goes up on a mountainside to pray, to spend time alone with the Father. His three-year ministry was punctuated by frequent withdrawals from his disciples and the crowds to hear the still, small voice of the Father.

We, too, need to exercise that same discipline—every day—if we want to discern God's voice. For very busy people, the secret to accomplishing this is to schedule the time. Yes, I know it sounds strange to write God onto the appointment calendar. However, much like making sure we schedule time to commute to work, read the newspaper, cook dinner, and go to the gym for our workouts, spending meaningful time with God requires setting the time aside and carefully guarding those periods.

Too often we're content with sponge-bath prayer, dabbing ourselves by saying grace before dinner or praying briefly during a worship service. Instead, we need to immerse ourselves daily in the shower of prayer.

If you're as much of a slave to a daily planner as I am, schedule *at least* ten to fifteen minutes each day to talk with God. If you're a student or someone employed outside of the home, try to set that time aside early in the day, before your schedule becomes less manageable. Perhaps that's before you leave home in the morning. If you travel a lot, try to set aside time early each day in your hotel room. If you're a stay-at-home parent, do this when the kids are napping or when they have gone out the door to school. Make this a part of your schedule every day for three weeks. (People who study human behavior say that, for some strange reason, doing something for twenty-one days straight helps it become a habit.)

If you have a long commute, you may be tempted to spend this discerning time with God in the car, bus, or train. Resist that temptation because there are too many distractions. I know from experience the downside of trying to talk to God while commuting. For sixteen years I drove to and from a job in downtown Los Angeles, a commute that took about two-and-a-half hours round trip. Although that was a productive time for prayer talking *to* God, especially prayers of petition for people and concerns on my prayer list, it was difficult to hear God's voice among the freeway noise and the continual distraction of drivers making sudden lane changes. Plus, it was a challenge to keep my fingers from straying to the radio "on" button.

If possible, find a quiet spot at home that you can consistently come back to and where you can settle into prayer. Moses had such a place called the Tent of Meeting, where he went during the years he led God's people through the desert toward the Promised Land. Something wondrous happened every time Moses entered it: "As Moses went into the tent, the pillar of cloud would come down and stay at the entrance, while the LORD spoke with Moses. . . . The LORD would speak to Moses face to face, as a man speaks with his friend" (Exodus. 33:9, 11).

Picture yourself face-to-face with God in your own Tent of Meeting. And keep coming back every day.

The second component to hearing God's voice is to ask and listen. Ask God for direction and then listen intently. This may sound incredibly obvious, but how many of us really do this when we pray? From the moment our feet hit the floor in the morning to the time our head hits the pillow at night, we are bombarded with noise, needs, deadlines, and distractions. It's difficult to settle into the peace and quiet required to hear God.

This can be accomplished partly by the location we choose, but it's also dependant upon our willingness to empty our minds of the things that get us all wound up each day. This takes some practice.

As I deliberated whether God was calling me to leave my job, I found it helpful to go through three distinct stages in prayer. I still make use of them:

- Forced quiet,
- Asking questions,
- Listening for answers.

Forced quiet

In this initial stage I purposefully try to push every extraneous thought out of my mind. That's tough at first. Initially, my mind sometimes drifts to silly things like that day's to-do list, last night's Lakers game, or even a song that was playing on the radio when I woke up. Don't feel guilty or concerned when that happens. It's natural. Just work through it by settling down into the moment and reminding yourself why you're doing this—to help you latch onto just a small portion of the mind of God and what God wants to share with you.

If you continue to be distracted, ask God to help you settle down into the conversation. I sometimes find it helpful to start this quiet time by slowly saying "Lord, I come before you to hear you and do your will." Repeat that a few times as you settle into prayer. Clear your mind so you can concentrate on God and your intimate time together with him. After all, meaningful conversations require us to focus closely on the one with whom we're speaking.

Asking questions

After quieting your mind, bring your questions to God. This time may be a time when you wrestle with God a bit, bringing your concerns and your fears about where you think God might be leading you. Just as God allowed Jacob to wrestle with him, God will permit you to do the same thing, especially on something as important as your life's direction.

Listening for answers

You should set aside the most time for the third stage of your prayer-and-discernment step. That's the listening for answers time. If you are purposeful in the first two stages, you'll be amazed at how much easier it becomes to hear God's answers. Since God doesn't speak in an audible voice today, in this third and final stage of discerning prayer pay particular attention to thoughts, impressions, feelings, and senses. If possible, record them in a journal or in the last chapter of this book. Each day, see which thoughts and impressions return in your discerning prayer time. That's where journaling can be helpful. Pay special attention to those ideas that recur and seem to grow stronger. Never react immediately to a sense—even a strong one—that enters your mind one day. (In other words, don't quit your job because of a strong feeling you had in your prayer time that day.) Keep testing God on what you think he is saying to you.

As you try to discern what you think God is telling you, start testing things out using the remaining steps of discernment outlined later in this chapter.

What's most important in discerning prayer is to resist coming into the throne room of God with your own agenda. This prayer time is not intended for you to go through a list of demands for God, merely asking him to bless what you want to do. That's a shortcut to failure, and it will short circuit the rest of *The Jonah Factor* steps. Instead, come before God with an open heart and a willingness to do what God wants. That obedient attitude activates a promise Jesus makes to us in Matthew 7 when he says, "Ask and it will be given to you; seek and you will find; knock and the door will be opened to you. For everyone who asks, receives; he who seeks, finds; and to him who knocks, the door will be opened."

Think of discerning prayer as tuning in a radio station. Amidst all the static and channels on the dial, you're looking for a particular station. Unless you have that station preset, you'll need to search a bit. Once you lock in on it, you'll need to minimize the background noise in the room or car. Perhaps you'll put on a headset to hear better. You'll turn up the volume. And then you'll listen.

You might not understand how a radio is able to tune in a transmission from hundreds of miles away and bring it to you so clearly; you just know that it works. It's the same way with prayer. We might not completely understand how it is we can communicate with God in such an intimate manner in our very own Tent of Meeting; all we know is that we can and that God hears us just as we can hear him.

Much like radio, prayer is a very personal encounter. Garrison Keillor, the clever, soft-spoken host of "A Prairie Home Companion," once described the medium of radio as "so intimate, it's embarrassing to think about."

That's what we strive for in discerning prayer, an intimate time with God in which we can hear his voice prompting us regarding what to do. Prayer is the link bringing us into close partnership with our Lord, or as theologian Dallas Willard writes in *The Divine Conspiracy,* "the most adequate description of prayer is simply, 'Talking to God about what we are doing together'" (San Francisco: HarperCollins, 1997, p. 243).

Prayer moves us from "MY will be done" to "THY will be done."

In this important step, we're also looking for the strength and peace that will encourage us to align our work with God's will. It's a serenity promised in Philippians 4:6-7, "Do not be anxious about anything, but in everything, by prayer and petition, with thanksgiving, present your requests to God. And the peace of God, which transcends all understanding, will guard your hearts and minds in Christ Jesus."

One more thought regarding Step 1: If you're not already a member of a congregation, ask God to lead you to one. Pray about it and start visiting some in your area as part of your discernment. Its importance will become more evident in Step 6.

Although prayer girds us for discerning God's voice, it also should be integrated into each of the remaining twelve steps of *The Jonah Factor*.

In other words, "pray continuously" (1 Thessalonians 5:17).

Reflection Point

Key thought

> *Prayer is the most obvious and most difficult of the 13 Steps in* The Jonah Factor *process. Perhaps that's because most of us measure our daily prayer time in seconds, not minutes. Yet, hearing God's voice in prayer will be critical for you to discern God's direction for your life, forming the foundation upon which the remaining twelve steps of* The Jonah Factor *are built.*

Questions

1. How much time do you spend in prayer each day? What would it take to increase that time?
   - ❏ More purposefully set the time aside for prayer
   - ❏ Develop a better daily routine that integrates prayer throughout the day
   - ❏ Spend less time on recreational activities, like watching TV
   - ❏ Find a quiet place to pray, with less distractions
   - ❏ See firsthand the benefits of increasing prayer time

2. During prayer, do you have difficulty clearing your mind and focusing on God? What distracting thoughts or ideas come to mind while you're trying to pray?

3. Read the following guidelines. Develop a plan that puts them into action in your prayer life.
   • Carve out a half hour today or tomorrow.
   • Select a quiet place where there's little chance of interruption.
   • Enter into the three stages of prayer described in this chapter: 1) Forced quiet; 2) Asking questions; and 3) Listening for answers.
   • Take your time in each stage; don't move on to the next stage until you've settled effectively into the previous one.
   • Ask God questions about your work and what path God would like you to pursue.
   Try not to bring your own agenda into this prayer time, asking God simply to bless that.

4. Step 1 of *The Jonah Factor* is intended to help you discern God's thoughts; its goal is to show you God's plans in the work you do and to instill the confidence for you to follow his leading. That's going to take some time. Although this process will most likely take longer—perhaps far longer—than a week, for the next six days follow the same process for prayer as outlined in this chapter. Afterward, record your thoughts, impressions, and feelings.

Day 1:

Day 2:

Day 3:

Day 4:

Day 5:

Day 6:

Day 7:

5. As you look back on your notes, what thoughts, impressions, and feelings recurred most frequently? Record them in the journal, starting on page 178.

6. As you continue to pray while engaged in the rest of *The Jonah Factor* steps, record any strong impressions that occur to you in your prayer time. Continue to refine what you think God is showing you. Continue to seek discernment in prayer and refer to the thoughts you've already written down. Record the strongest impressions in the Step 1 section of the journal on page 178.

Step 2: Meditate on Scripture
Look to the Bible for revelation

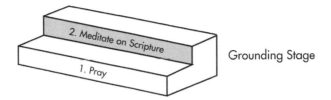

Grounding Stage

When I worked in the mutual fund industry I enjoyed reading a column that ran every few months in the *Wall Street Journal*. In it, a variety of financial advisers and investment professionals made predictions regarding what the stock market indexes would do in upcoming months. A few months later, their predictions would be compared to what would have happened if an investor had merely put pages of stock market listings on a wall and thrown darts, picking those stocks that the darts landed on.

That's similar to how some of us try to figure out God's will. We pull out a Bible, close our eyes, randomly open to a page, and then point our finger on the page. The verse under that finger is the one we assume God is using to speak to us. (Heaven help us, if we accidentally open to the book of Leviticus!)

God's revelation isn't a Magic 8-Ball®, and God doesn't speak to us through fortune cookies. Neither is it appropriate to approach the Bible in such a haphazard fashion. God is revealed to us progressively as we spend time with God and seek wisdom by reading Scripture carefully, thoughtfully, and prayerfully.

Although peppering your Bible with darts or pointed fingers won't get you closer to knowing the direction God wants you to move, there will be times, perhaps many, when a verse or two will jump off the pages because they seem to speak to something you've been wrestling with. That was true in my journey. My greatest heartburn was trying to figure out why I was sensing God moving me away from a corporate career in which I had been successful for almost thirty years. Why would God want me to restructure myself out of a job without having a job waiting at another company? Or, worse yet, why would God want me to wave goodbye to a corporate life that had treated me so well?

The answer came to me in—of all books—Revelation. I don't know exactly what prompted me to open to that section of the Bible; it's not one that I had frequently referred to for guidance, given its apocalyptic and sometimes confusing, symbolic writing. However, in my devotion time I was drawn to the closing chapters of the book of Revelation, especially chapter 21, where two verses hit me because they confirmed a strong sense I had developed in my discerning prayer time (Step 1). Verses 5 and 6 jumped out at me, as I read: "He who was seated on the throne said, 'I am making everything new!' Then he said, 'Write this down, for these words are trustworthy and true.' He said to me: 'It is done. I am the Alpha and the Omega, the Beginning and the End. To him who is thirsty I will give a drink without cost from the spring of the water of life.'"

That was it! With those words I sensed God assuring me that what I was discerning more and more strongly in my prayer time was, indeed, correct. God was trying to create something new in me, and I could trust God in all he was doing. I also took to heart the promise in verse 7 that God would provide for me and my family by giving us "a drink without cost," something that, indeed, came true repeatedly after I left my employer and generous salary.

As instructed in those verses, I literally did "write this down," and I taped those verses on my computer monitor to remind me of the promise and as an encouragement whenever I got cold feet and started doubting the path God had put me on.

I clung to that revelation from Revelation during the early stages of my transition into doing what God was calling me to do. As I proceeded to disconnect from my corporate job—and paycheck—I held on to that promise, never to be disappointed in having placed my trust in our Lord.

Searching the pages of Scripture also gave me tremendous encouragement when I was tempted to depart from the plan that was unfolding before me. At one point, several months after leaving my job (as the continuing lack of income caused me to start doubting God's plan), I began to engage in discussions regarding some corporate management opportunities that others called me about. One executive showed interest in having me come in for interviews for one of those positions. However, during my prayer, reflection, and Scripture time one morning, I came across the verses in Isaiah 43, in which God says: "Forget the former things; do not dwell on the past. See, I am doing a new thing! Now it springs up; do you not perceive it?" I took it as a not-so-subtle reminder to stop allowing myself to be distracted by the allure of taking the easy way out of my adventure.

It's no accident that 2 Timothy 3:16-17 tells us, "All scripture is inspired by God and is useful for teaching, for reproof, for correction, and for training in righteousness, so that everyone who belongs to God may be proficient, equipped for every good work"(NRSV). Through my reading of Scripture, God was clearly speaking to me, teaching me as I searched for answers, rebuking me when I wavered in my commitment to move forward with the plan, correcting me when I tried to insert my wants and needs into the equation, and training me for what lay ahead.

The key point to Step 2 is to take time—at least ten minutes (preferably more)—each day to read the Bible and to reflect on what you've studied. Pondering that day's readings is critical. Don't just read and move on. Throughout the day, linger on what you've read.

Many of us aren't Bible scholars, and it's daunting to think of spending that much time in a book that can sometimes be difficult to read and understand. If you're not accustomed to cracking open the pages of Scripture, here are some thoughts to get you started:

Find a good translation. Though many of us grew up with the old King James Version of the Bible, there are at least a half dozen more modern translations, including the New King James (NKJV), New Revised Standard (NRSV), the easy-to-read Contemporary English Version (CEV), and my favorite New International Version (NIV). One caution in settling on a translation: Avoid using books like *The Message* by Eugene Peterson as your sole Scripture reading source. Although an excellent book that uses modern-day English, complete with slang and current vernacular, *The Message* is a loose translation or paraphrase of the Scriptures. It is a valuable resource, when you're trying to understand particularly difficult sections, but use one of the other translations as your primary source.

Use a Study Bible. Once you've found a readable translation, look for one that includes study helps. These Bible versions usually contain notes and illustrations explaining what the writer meant, what customs or practices might have been prevalent, or what historical events were occurring at the time. The study notes found in these Bibles can be helpful in understanding context, a critical element in Bible study. You'll find that some sections of Scripture, especially in the Old Testament, are more veiled to modern-day readers because the customs and vernacular during the times in which they were written are so different than our own.

Here, my caution would be to avoid using the study notes as replacements for reading the actual Scripture. In fact, try not to read the study notes on the page unless you're having difficulty understanding the text. Oftentimes the Holy Spirit will help you understand even difficult-to-read Scripture passages without having to read the notes. We're looking for revelation in Step 2, and we want to give the Holy Spirit enough maneuvering space to reveal God's word to us. Use the study notes only when you get stuck on a passage for an extended period or as historical background once you've read a section of Scripture.

Pick a section of the Bible and start reading. The Bible consists of many books, some of which are more difficult for a novice to read than others. Some books are intimidating indeed. Where do you begin? If you haven't spent much time in this amazing, inspired Word of God, here are some hints to get you started:

If your goal is to read the entire Bible, the best place to start is in the New Testament. I recommend that people new to the experience start with the book of John, remembering that in the first chapter, every time John uses the term "the Word," he's referring to Jesus. Then read, in order, the books of Matthew, Mark, Luke, and the rest of the New Testament. Revelation, the last book of the Bible, is filled with apocalyptic images that have been interpreted in many ways. The first time through focus on the hope-filled message of the book. Read it as God's way of encouraging you to grow in faith and to trust that God will be present with you as you head into a new future. Look also at the wonderful praise language in Revelation.

After finishing the New Testament, dig into the Old Testament, starting with Genesis and reading through the rest of it, book by book. When we've read the New Testament, parts of the Old Testament make even more sense, especially when we are introduced to the God who calls people and saves them. We also recognize how some of the prophets point to a coming Messiah and how those prophecies are fulfilled in Jesus. Books such as Leviticus, Numbers, and Deuteronomy are long and filled with laws and lists that may not seem relevant, but I encourage you not to skip them as they contain valuable history and some interesting nuggets. Just keep reading through.

Be faithful in studying the Bible every day. About ten years ago, I set out to read it cover to cover. I had been told that it would be impossible for me to really understand the God *of* the Bible until I looked for the God *in* the Bible. Indeed, that was true.

It took me about a year and a half the first time through. What an amazing journey that was, revealing things that I would have never understood in a lifetime of listening to sermons, reading devotion books, tuning in to Christian radio, or even attending seminary. Throughout that time I had the strong sense of God's specific revelation to me. Granted, it takes discipline to spend time each day in Scripture, but God honors that commitment and follow-through by showing us things we wouldn't otherwise see or experience. That's why reading the Bible is so important in *The Jonah Factor* steps, second only to discerning prayer.

One other thought on this step. If you repeatedly have difficulty trying to understand what God may be saying to you through Scripture, try using a Bible commentary or a daily devotional book to accompany your readings. There are dozens of excellent devotion books on the market, aimed at people from almost every walk of life and background—busy housewives, teenagers, new believers, seasoned Christians, businesspeople, and others. You're also welcome to check out daily devotions I write, called *Digging Deeper* (available at www.digging-deeper.com), which help readers reflect on the weekly Bible readings read in worship at many mainstream Christian churches. A collection of devotions I have often turned to is an older but popular book called *My Utmost for His Highest* by Oswald Chambers. It's been especially useful to me in trying to discern God's will.

Reflection Point

Key thought
> *While prayer allows us to align ourselves with God's will, reading Scripture is a way in which God and his hopes and dreams for us are revealed. Spend at least ten minutes each day in the Bible and see how God is revealed to you and how God's plans for you begin to unfold.*

Questions
1. What is the most remarkable revelation you've ever had in reading the Bible? How did it affect your life?

2. For the next week spend at least ten minutes (preferably longer) each day reading from the Bible. Follow the guidelines in this chapter regarding where to start and how to progress.

3. As you engage in this process of reading Scripture, integrate what you read with whatever you're sensing during prayer time. Record your insights below.

Day 1:

Day 2:

Day 3:

Day 4:

Day 5:

Day 6:

Day 7:

4. As you look back on the notes you wrote following your prayer time over the previous week, what thoughts, impressions, and feelings recurred most frequently? Record them in the Step 2 section of the journal on page 179.

• •

Step 3: Examine Your Passions
Be aware of a shift in your interests

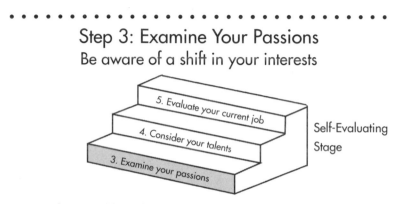

5. Evaluate your current job

4. Consider your talents

3. Examine your passions

Self-Evaluating Stage

Some of us are blessed with jobs and careers we love. Going to work is a joy, not a requirement. Sometimes it's even too much of a source of pleasure and identity, causing us to neglect more important parts of our lives, including our relationships with God, family, and friends. Nonetheless, when our God-given talents and interests correspond with our careers or occupations, it's a match made in heaven.

My father-in-law has been blessed for a lifetime in his career. He often says he can't believe people pay him to have so much fun. His name is Wink Martindale. Many of you might recognize that distinctive name. He's a game show host, radio announcer, voiceover artist, and a frequent master of ceremonies at countless charity dinners and telethons. Wink loves what he's doing. He started as a radio announcer in his teens and is still hard at work in his seventies using the gifts— especially that amazing voice—that God has blessed him with.

I envy Wink. He's been able to use pretty much the same talents throughout his life, building upon his skills and reputation without interruption. And he's had an amazing string of successes in an often unforgiving, cutthroat industry, one in which he has boldly proclaimed his faith.

However, most of us aren't blessed with that kind of longevity in the work we do. Studies show that Americans change career direction three to four times during their working lives—not just job changes, but often career transformations. There's no evidence to suggest that most of these people are following God's call in making those adjustments. Perhaps they're hearing a call they don't quite understand, but they're following it anyway, going more with gut instinct.

Regardless, God often does purposefully prompt us into a different direction in different seasons of our life.

Look at the apostle known as Paul. He was a powerful religious leader at the time of Jesus in the first century, a member of the Jewish group known as the Pharisees. He actually participated in trying to put a stop to a small but growing band of Jesus' followers. But when Paul had a spiritual encounter with the risen Lord Jesus Christ on the Damascus Road, he was changed forever. He left his prominent calling to become a theologian, pastor, and evangelist of the newly emerging Christian movement. Had he followed the original map of his life, he would likely have gone to his grave a Pharisee, but he was receptive to God's call, even though it required him to make a dramatic shift in career, thinking, and lifestyle, and he became arguably the greatest Christian evangelist.

Something stirs deep within us when God is preparing us to do something different. One way God gets us ready for the changes ahead is by prompting a shift in our interests. The change is often subtle at first, perhaps as simple as a new interest in a certain subject or topic or a desire to dig more deeply into something that has never intrigued us before.

For me, the shift wasn't immediately apparent. In fact, only in retrospect did I notice the seeds that God was planting. In my move up the career ladder, one of the responsibilities I had to let go of was my writing. I had done considerable writing in earlier jobs, but as my management responsibilities increased there simply wasn't enough time to write. So I delegated more and more of that to my staff.

However, even before my more formal discernment process began, I had an increasing desire to write. To refresh those skills that had been dormant for a few years I pulled several books on writing off my bookshelf. They included Brenda Ueland's classic on writing and the creative process, *If You Want to Write,* a book that transcends the craft of writing and examines the issue of how our work should reflect our passions. I hadn't looked at those books in years. Up to that point, my reading time usually revolved around management tomes by well known CEOs or biographies of great leaders.

Interestingly, my desire to write didn't include the dozens of sales and marketing publications my department produced. Instead, my aspiration was to write about issues of faith and to use my skills to help people understand how rich the Bible is in addressing issues of daily life. That interest ultimately led me to developing *Digging Deeper,* the publication of daily devotions I mentioned earlier.

Once again, the initial spark of interest grew into something far bigger than I could have imagined. A publication that started out as a homemade and homely little insert into our congregation's weekly worship service bulletin is today read by thousands of subscribers across the United States. I never imagined how successful *Digging Deeper* would be; all I did was follow my passions.

One important note on this topic: Being passionate about your vocation doesn't mean you'll enjoy every aspect of it. Even the most rewarding work sometimes requires working with difficult people on demanding projects with problematic deadlines. The work for which you have a passion won't necessarily be perfect, but your delight in what you're doing will significantly outweigh whatever challenges you encounter. Often that satisfaction will come from knowing that your work serves a great purpose, one for which you were specifically created.

Reflection Point

Key thought

> *The key to harnessing our passions to a specific vocation is to determine whether it melds our skills and talents with God's greater purpose. We may mistakenly assume that the right vocation is one we'll enjoy or feel passionate about at every moment. Although it won't make the troublesome aspects of our work go away, our passion for it will validate that it's the right thing for us to do.*

Questions

1. What do you enjoy most about the work you currently do?

2. How has your enjoyment of the work you do increased, decreased, or stayed the same in the past year?

3. Have you noticed a shift in interests? Are you realizing that you never had a deep interest in your work?

4. What is God showing you in Steps 1 and 2 that causes you to question your passion for or commitment to the work you're currently doing? If so, what have you discerned so far?

5. In what kind of work, job, or field of study can you picture yourself enjoying the work so much that you'd lose track of time?

6. Do you sense God calling you to stay in the work you're doing? If not, in what new direction do you feel God nudging you?

7. As you reflect on your work-related passions, record your thoughts in the Step 3 section of the journal on page 179.

. . . .

Step 4: Consider your talents
Be sensitive to changes in your skills

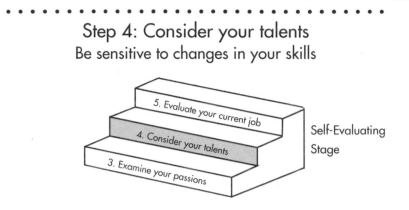

There's a curious passage in the Old Testament book of Daniel, chapter 4. King Nebuchadnezzar is strolling on the roof of his Babylonian palace. He looks around, marveling at the fruits of his skills, saying, "Is not this the great Babylon I have built as the royal residence, by my mighty power and for the glory of my majesty?" (4:29-30).

But here's the strange part: those words are still on Nebuchadnezzar's lips when God tells him that he's about to take away the talents that have made the king so successful. Here's what happens: "Immediately what had been said about Nebuchadnezzar was fulfilled. He was driven away from people and ate grass like cattle. His body was drenched with the dew of heaven until his hair grew like the feathers of an eagle and his nails like the claws of a bird" (Daniel 4:33).

God knocked the king down a few rungs—so many, in fact, that his behavior was no longer human. He was nose-down in the field, chewing cud with the cows.

In a way, that's how I started to feel. As I searched Scripture and tried to discern the direction God was leading me, a question kept coming to mind: Why was I suddenly having difficulty grasping things in my profession that I had understood clearly for many years?

I had been employed in the mutual fund business for almost ten years and in the banking industry for another six years. At work, I had been exposed to the concepts of investing, money management, and economics that drive these businesses. Yet, increasingly,

I couldn't remember the details of some of these concepts or retain new information. I began noticing this during one high-profile project, as my firm was preparing to roll out a new pricing structure for its mutual funds. What previously had been easy for me to learn and remember was now incredibly difficult—simple stuff, really—threatening my effectiveness as a vice president in the unit that had to produce the sales and marketing materials to accompany the rollout.

At first, I imagined that I was in the early stages of Alzheimer's disease, which took my father's life. Too often, I felt as dumb as Nebuchadnezzar grazing in the fields. I would walk out of meetings asking members of my staff about some of the details of the rollout and the conclusions we had arrived at, and increasingly I was reluctant to make decisions because I feared they would be the wrong ones.

However, I noticed that this disorientation didn't extend into other areas, especially those that dealt with church-related projects I was involved in, including the increased public speaking I was doing on faith-related topics at church and the daily devotions I was writing.

In spite of my difficulties at work, somehow I was able to learn, process, and retain sophisticated spiritual concepts and write and speak about them. While my staff at the office was probably scratching their heads, wondering why I was so indecisive, my *Digging Deeper* readers were sending me e-mails and thank-you notes telling me how much they were learning from my daily devotions and how certain ones touched them deeply.

I was munching on grass at work while I was dining on filet mignon in my other, even more complicated, endeavors. Long-suffering Job exclaimed, "The LORD gave and the LORD has taken away" (Job 1:21). I experienced that firsthand. Where previously God had blessed me with a good grasp of business and the ability to learn new things, I found myself increasingly anxious about my inability to "get it." The talents and abilities God had given me during an earlier season of life were diminishing to prepare me for the next one.

An important element of the 13 Steps of *The Jonah Factor* is to take an inventory of where you are in your career, education, or even retirement. It's important to reflect on whether your talents and abilities are shifting and whether God is still blessing what you're doing by providing the talents and the mental resources to continue. Although subtle at first, a shift in your abilities may help confirm that God is trying to move you in a different direction.

Reflection Point

Key thought

Very few of us were destined to remain at the same job for our entire lifetimes. God often changes the plan. We need to maintain the flexibility to both sense those changes and then be obedient in following them. So, how do you know when it's time to move on to something else? Often that's signaled by a shift in your talents and abilities.

Questions

1. What are some of your more unique talents and abilities? To properly use that talent or ability (as well as others), would it be best to stay with your current work or should you start looking for something else?

2. Have you noticed a decrease in any skills or talents, especially recently?

3. Have you developed—or wanted to develop—any new skills, abilities, or insights recently? What are they? What talents and abilities would you most like to develop and use in the work you do? What type of work would best allow you to utilize those talents and abilities? Compare that with what you've been discerning in the previous three steps of *The Jonah Factor* process and record it in the Step 4 section of the journal on page 180.

Step 5: Evaluate Your Current Job
Determine whether your work is invigorating or exhausting

It's no secret that we're invigorated when engaging in activities we enjoy. It's the stuff we dislike that saps us of energy. However, there's more to it. When we are doing exactly what God has called us to do, we're in harmony with God, and he provides us with the necessary stamina.

Let's look again at the life of Paul. Following his conversion, Paul went on at least three lengthy missionary journeys to spread the gospel and plant churches. He covered thousands of miles on foot or by boat. During his travels, he withstood persecution, imprisonment, chronic illness, and rebellious church members. Yet nowhere in Scripture do we find Paul complaining about exhaustion. Sure, there are times when he's fatigued, he suffers from a "thorn in the flesh," he shows exasperation, and he's sometimes short-tempered. However, we still see vitality in Paul that surpasses our expectations, especially considering the grueling schedule he kept and the difficulties he encountered.

That's the Holy Spirit's power at work. In Acts 1:8, Jesus promises his followers that "you will receive power when the Holy Spirit comes to you." Paul was a recipient of that power because his journeys were fulfilling what God intended for him to do. God replenished whatever energy drained out of Paul in his work to spread the gospel.

There was a parallel in my life as I tried early on to work through *The Jonah Factor*'s 13 Steps. At the time I was in a demanding job that required fifty to sixty hours a week. On top of that, I had a long daily commute and a moderate business travel schedule. At the same time I was president of our congregation's church council, a responsibility that required considerable time, especially whenever we had church council meetings or special activities.

During the two years I was council president, I noticed something strange: My full-time job exhausted me while my church activities energized me. Common sense would tell us that it should have been the other way around, that my leadership role on church council would have been the straw that broke the camel's back, but it didn't.

Our council meetings were held once a month, usually on a Wednesday night. By that point in the week my energy would be on the downslide as my early wakeups, long commutes, back-to-back office meetings and long workdays began to sap my energy. On top of that, council meetings usually lasted several hours as we wrangled with issues that couldn't be confined to sound-bite discussions. Those meetings would often go past midnight and occasionally continue until 1 A.M. or so. By that point I had been awake for more than twenty hours.

However, by the end of those council meetings I had more energy than when I had started the day, and that vigor continued into the next day, in spite of my only being able to grab a few hours of sleep that night. I had a growing sense of where that energy was coming from. Clearly, I wasn't drawing that vigor from deep inside of me. I continually tried that at the office—usually augmented by substantial doses of caffeine and sugar—and was rarely successful. I realized, over time, that this renewal was coming directly from God. In fact, often when I would return home after very late church council meetings my wife, Lyn, would roll over in bed and ask how it went. My response invariably was, "I can't explain it, but I've still got so much energy. That must be God's faithfulness."

While my career was sucking energy out of me, my responsibilities at church required the Holy Spirit to pump it back in. And that's exactly what happened!

Step 5 of *The Jonah Factor* requires some thinking about whether the position you're employed in, your course of study at school, or the activities you're engaged in at home or in retirement are energy sappers or energy enhancers.

One important sign of whether God is blessing your activities is whether the Holy Spirit is replenishing what the work takes out of you.

Reflection Point

Key thought

When we're working at what we were uniquely created to do, God's Spirit provides the stamina required to get the job done. Once our energy and enthusiasm consistently wane, however, that's often a signal that God is calling us to do something different. So how much "oomph" do you have for your work?

Questions

1. How would you describe the energy level you have for your work?
   - ❑ Consistently high
   - ❑ Usually high
   - ❑ Moderate; it varies with what's going on
   - ❑ Frequently low
   - ❑ Always low; I have to force myself to do it

2. Looking back over the past year, would you say your energy level and enthusiasm for the work you're doing has:
   - ❑ Decreased
   - ❑ Increased
   - ❑ Stayed the same

3. If your energy level and enthusiasm for your work has increased or stayed the same (provided it was moderate to high to begin with), you might already be doing appropriate work. However, if your energy level on the job has decreased, why do you think that has happened?
   - ❑ I'm bored
   - ❑ My work isn't very fulfilling
   - ❑ It seems like I've been doing this for an awfully long time

- ❏ My interests have changed
- ❏ My work is physically demanding, and I no longer have the energy

4. For what job or specific work do you think you'd have greater enthusiasm? What kind of work excites you?

5. Reflect on your answers above, and record the type of vocation you think would energize you in the Step 5 section of the journal on page 180.

• •

Step 6: Commit to a Congregation
Become an active member

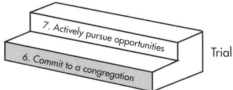

Most of us become consumers, not contributors, when we join a particular congregation. Our reasons for attending church have more to do with our needs and wants than our desire to serve God or enter into a more meaningful relationship with God and with other believers. We look to consume resources, kind of like going to the movies or a restaurant or a shopping mall. We go because we like what a particular church offers. Perhaps that's a dynamic pastor, priest, or minister who delivers interesting sermons. Or maybe it's a youth program that will provide our children with a moral foundation. Or we like that congregation because we're lonely and its members are friendly.

We conducted a survey at our church a number of years ago asking members to tell us what prompted them to visit and then join the congregation. The number one answer from respondents was that they had friends, neighbors, or family members who attended our church, and that drew them into the fold. Far down the list was the idea of becoming a member because felt they would be best able to serve God there.

There's nothing wrong with joining a church body in order to be with people with whom we like to worship and where we can be fed spiritually. But that's only half of the role a congregation should play in our walk with Christ. An equally important component is to be challenged and nurtured in the steps we should be taking to grow in faith and to serve God by serving others.

If you're not a member of a congregation, make it a high priority to seek out and join one. And hopefully you've been praying for God to guide you toward the right church as part of Step 1.

Here are some issues to think about as you look for a church:

1. *Is it fairly close to home?* Worship service attendance and involvement in church activities drops the farther away we live. The reason is simple: Few of us want to add a lengthy commute to the time we spend at church, especially in metropolitan areas where so much time is already spent on the road. Try to find a church location fifteen minutes or less from your home.

2. *Is it a welcoming congregation?* You can get a pretty good feel on your first visit about the kind of members who belong to that church. If they're open and hospitable, you'll know it right away. Many churches have "ambassadors" whose responsibility is to greet newcomers and make them feel comfortable on their first and second visits. That's a good sign of what kind of environment they're trying to foster. You'll probably want to steer away from a church whose members form tight cliques between worship services and make you feel like an outsider, or whose members leave the premises immediately after a worship service ends. Observe how people interact with one another and whether members come up to you when you stand alone or as a family near the coffee maker or the food court.

3. *Are the teachings of that congregation consistent with Scripture?*
    This may be difficult to determine early on, especially if you're
    not that familiar with what's written in the Bible. However, it's
    important to find a church that will support your search for
    the truth and for how God is leading you. Listen for a consis-
    tent focus on the gospel that is seeking, speaking, and teaching
    that truth so you can apply it to your life. One indication of
    a congregation's openness to God's truth is its willingness to
    allow members to test its preachings and teachings by what the
    Bible says about important topics.

4. *Is the congregation committed to helping you understand
    which gifts God has blessed you with and helping you develop
    them?* Romans 12:4-8 gives us insight into some of God's
    gifts—teaching, encouraging, helping others, prophesying,
    leading, and showing mercy. An excellent congregation will
    help its members understand what those gifts are, which of
    them they have and how to best serve God with them. This
    area will be especially important as you try to work through
    most of the remaining *Jonah Factor* steps, especially Steps 7,
    10, and 11.

5. *Will you be challenged to grow in faith?* Few of us chal-
    lenge ourselves sufficiently in our faith walk. It's so easy to
    be self-satisfied and focused on the success of our baby steps
    that we often stop there, unwilling to stretch and take on
    the more challenging work God intends. Does the congrega-
    tion you're considering have formal or informal mentoring
    programs or accountability groups? Without others to hold
    our feet to the fire—in loving ways, of course—we often
    stagnate in our walk, content with how far we've come and
    missing opportunities for an even deeper and more mean-
    ingful relationship with Christ and a greater sense of serving
    God's purpose.

6. *Are there a variety of small groups, especially if you're consider-ing joining a large congregation?* Belonging to a congregation of, say, more than one thousand members is a mixed bless-ing. On one hand most large churches offer a greater variety of worship services (traditional, contemporary, multilingual), programs, and activities. They often provide childcare and have dynamic youth programs. Many offer life-stage ministries, helping members as they transition from youth to young adult to working adult to retirement. On the other hand, large con-gregations can be lonely places, especially for new members. Although their worship services can be inspiring, we might feel lost in the crowd. Small groups are a helpful outgrowth of size issues at many larger congregations. They come in the form of Bible studies, accountability groups, service groups whose members take on projects ranging from mission trips to feeding the hungry, and retirement groups that engage in fun activities or travel. Small groups help a large church feel like a small one. Plus, they're critical to your spiritual growth, as we'll see in Step 9.

7. *Is there a comfortable fit?* Each of us looks for something differ-ent in our worship experience and in the people with whom we want to worship and serve God. Some of us prefer more tradi-tional candles and stained glass places of worship, while others are more inspired in modern, warehouse-like settings. When our daughter Hannah was in the process of selecting a college we received some helpful advice. We were told to have her stand in the middle of a college campus, look around slowly, and soak in the atmosphere. Beyond the curriculum, prestige, pos-sible scholarships, and social life, we were told to ask her what feeling she got from each campus. We were encouraged to ask her the question, "Can I picture myself attending this school?" That was good advice, and it's the same sense we should try to develop before we choose a church or congregation.

If you don't already have a good church home, selecting a good "home church" is critical to your progression through *The Jonah Factor* process. It will be the platform upon which you'll want to grow your faith, gain encouragement, and try some new things, all necessary elements to determining what God is calling you to do.

One note here, however: In spite of your best efforts, you might find it difficult to integrate yourself into a specific congregation. For whatever reason—size, structure, personalities of congregants—you might not mesh completely with any of the congregations you're considering. Don't let that dissuade you from at least finding a group of fellow believers in which you can try out some of the things described in later steps. Perhaps you're most comfortable with a particular Bible study group or Christian men's or women's group, one in which your faith is nurtured and whose members will help you take the steps in faith toward discerning the job or activity God is calling you to. Even if you're not completely comfortable with the church you've selected, continue to attend worship services there, and rely on your small group to help you grow in faith and test out what God shows you.

Reflection Point

Key thought

Most Americans know how to be good consumers. In fact, we're so skilled at it that we often apply the standards of consumerism to how we select a church. We join because we want to be served, not because we want to serve. However, one of the greatest blessings of active involvement in a church is the opportunity for growing through worship, learning, and service. This is a key Jonah Factor *step.*

Questions

1. If you are a member or regularly attend a church, how active are you in the life of that congregation?
   - ❑ Occasionally attend worship services at my church
   - ❑ I attend church regularly
   - ❑ I participate in some church activities in addition to regularly attending church
   - ❑ I participate in or contribute to one or more ministries at my church
   - ❑ I am actively involved in my church by regularly attending weekly worship services and serving in one or more ministries there

2. If you're not participating regularly in a congregation, why is that?
   - ❑ I don't have time
   - ❑ Churchgoers are hypocritical
   - ❑ Going to church was boring
   - ❑ I haven't found a church I like
   - ❑ I don't know how to get started looking for a church

3. What would it take for you to become an active member of a congregation?
   - ❑ I'd have to find a group I really enjoy being with and would help me grow in faith
   - ❑ I'd have to reduce my other responsibilities or time constraints
   - ❑ I'd have to have some compelling reason, such as a good adult education program, exciting worship services, or day care for my children
   - ❑ I'd have to find a congregation that could help me understand God's plan for my life

4. If a congregation could help you develop one skill or talent that could be applied in work you'd like to do, what would it be? Record that in the Step 6 section of the journal on page 181.

• •

Step 7: Actively Pursue Opportunities
Try out some new ideas and talents

Trial Balloon Stage

Singer Whitney Houston was one of the so-called divas of popular music for much of the 1990s. Riding a giant wave of success throughout that decade, she was the first recording artist ever to have seven consecutive singles hit number one. Her 1993 remake of the Dolly Parton song, "I Will Always Love You," is said to have been the biggest hit single in rock-and-roll history. During most of the 1990s it was nearly impossible to scan the radio dial without coming across one of her songs.

Not many people know that Ms. Houston developed her voice, technique, and style at church. As a teenager she performed as a soloist in the junior gospel choir at New Hope Baptist Church in Newark, New Jersey. Interestingly, that's the same church choir that birthed another famous singer of an earlier era, her cousin Dionne Warwick.

Most churches are starving for people to contribute their time and talents—and not just in the choir. They need dedicated accountants to serve on finance committees, marketing people to help promote church events, event planners to help coordinate worship services and special activities, and people with leadership skills to serve as deacons or church council members.

Serving God through your congregation is a valuable endeavor. But there's an ulterior motive, as well. Volunteering your time and talents can help you develop and polish different skills in a safe environment, an important step in *The Jonah Factor* process. Here's why: If during this process you sense God calling you to do something different, you'll likely need to start developing different skills or using ones that may be a bit rusty.

And you won't often want to do that at your current place of work.

If you've made a commitment to a supportive congregation (see Step 6), you'll be able to offer your services and in the process help discern whether you have talent in the area God seems to be leading you toward. Much like Whitney Houston and Dionne Warwick did in developing their singing and performing styles, you'll be able to try some new things and experiment with what God is showing you in the discernment process—all in the safe environment of a loving congregation.

Step 7 takes advantage of one of the main purposes of the church—"to prepare God's people for works of service, so that the body of Christ may be built up" (Ephesians 4:12).

Think of your home church as an incubator. Most of us were born prematurely, perhaps not physically, but spiritually. Much like the "preemie" born before his or her lungs are properly developed, we come into this world insufficiently equipped to know God and to understand his will. While nurtured inside the incubator of a loving church, we're able to learn more about God and where God may be leading us, and we can develop the skills and talents God is calling us to use.

Here's how this step worked into my adventure. In addition to an interest in developing my writing skills, I developed a renewed interest in public speaking, something I had honed by joining Toastmasters International and being a member of my company's speakers' bureau many years before. At that time I was working for an aerospace firm whose primary program was the Space Shuttle, and I began to go out into the community and make presentations on the space program. I liked speaking in front of people.

As my faith deepened, however, I felt more and more drawn to writing and speaking on Christian topics. My congregation, Ascension Lutheran Church, was there to nurture me in this interest and to help me become a more effective writer and speaker. In addition to giving me the green light for my *Digging Deeper* publication, I was given opportunities to speak at a variety of church services and functions. Our men's ministry allowed me to deliver devotions at each of our monthly men's breakfasts and to be an occasional guest speaker. I gave temple talks to thousands of congregants, both at our church and others, followed by delivering sermons a few years later.

Frankly, my talks and devotions weren't always dazzling, as I tried out new ideas and different techniques. While in my church incubator, I took full advantage of the love and support I received in my new endeavors by sometimes pushing the limits, all in an attempt to discover and then sharpen my talents in new areas. There were times I stood in the pulpit at packed worship services where my knees shook and my hands trembled. I initially felt out of my element, perhaps because I hadn't yet studied at seminary. I hoped no one would notice. During other times, I could tell from the body language of the congregation that I wasn't making my point effectively. However, I knew at all times that I had the love and encouragement of the members of my congregation and that many considered themselves to be part of my adventure, gently helping me through the rough spots to get me where I needed to go.

There are countless other examples of how my congregation and its leadership provided opportunities to help me grow and then supported me. They were—and still are—partners in my journey of discernment. That's the power of the Holy Spirit working through God's earthly incubator, the church.

There's one other important element to Step 6: Do the best you can in whatever activity you engage in. Don't get sloppy just because this is "volunteer work." You're doing this not only to help your congregation live out its purpose as God's instrument in the world but also as a way for you to serve God and to test out your talents and abilities. Even in these volunteer activities, bring God your unblemished first fruits.

Reflection Point

Key thought

> *There is no more fertile ground for trying out new things than a supportive church. Most congregations welcome people using their gifts and talents to enliven the congregation and reach out to the world. A congregation can provide outstanding opportunities to test your wings in whatever work-related call God has placed on your life.*

Questions

1. What have you discerned so far regarding work God may be calling you to? How does doing this work involve learning and using new skills or at least adding on to skills you already have?

2. What opportunities exist within your congregation to try out skills that you might not otherwise have the chance to hone elsewhere?

3. Have you looked more closely at the ministries, committees, leadership positions, and programs at your church? What opportunities do you see to try out new skills that might be helpful in new work that God may be calling you to?

4. Most congregations have listings and descriptions of areas in which they encourage participation and service. Determine what area you'd like to focus on, again in an attempt to help you develop or refine your talents and skills. Write down the opportunity that most interests you in the Step 7 section of the journal on page 181. Then talk to someone in your congregation responsible for that area and volunteer your time.

- -

Step 8: Learn New Things
Augment your interest with knowledge

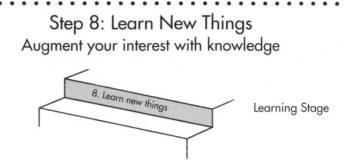

Learning Stage

New endeavors usually require training. Even staying in our current jobs involves learning new things, such as the latest computer software or new workplace processes.

If God is leading you to consider new work, it's possible that you'll need to develop far greater knowledge and abilities for the new venture God has planned for you. Chances are, though, that there will be one big difference between this training and any on-the-job instruction or other education in which you've participated in recent years—you'll love doing it!

Step 8 has to do with more than just figuring out what you'll need to learn to ensure a successful transition into a new job or career. It's also an important step to showing whether you're on the right track.

Here's how: Many of us begrudgingly take classes, attend seminars, or pursue advanced degrees because we believe they'll benefit our careers. In some fields, such as medical, legal, and financial, a certain number of continuing education classes are required each year to stay certified. In others, they provide opportunities for promotion. Dozens of my friends and coworkers over the years have earned MBAs, a two-year or more process that many described as pure hell. In most cases, they didn't view going after an MBA as an opportunity to learn something new. It was merely seen as a ticket to a promotion or, at least, a substantial pay raise over time.

Stop for a moment and reflect on what type of class or training would intrigue you sufficiently for you to give up your time and effort. Think outside the box. Don't assume that it has to be in your chosen field of work. What if you could attend any class right now? Would it be one that offers you an opportunity to learn a new language, develop a skill, or study something you've been curious about?

Now, does the class or training fit in any way with the direction you feel God leading you—even if not directly? If you've been thoughtful in following *The Jonah Factor* steps so far, you're probably starting to discern God's direction. Use Step 8 to confirm what you've been sensing.

For example, I once worked with a woman, Elizabeth, who had an increasing desire to run a restaurant—not to be a chef, mind you, just to run a restaurant. Now, restaurant management was a far cry from the project management position she held at our company. Her desire grew until she finally "relented" (her word, not mine) and took an adult education course at a local junior college. She loved it and was hooked from the opening moments of her first class. Elizabeth stuck with it and, a couple of years later, she left the company to pursue her dream, starting with turning around a struggling restaurant her son owned. This aggressive and successful project manager knew deep in her heart that she was called to do something different with her life. Taking that first class confirmed her talents and interest in that area and gave her the confidence to step onto an entirely different career track.

I had a similar experience in my discernment process. As I felt God calling me in a different direction, I developed an insatiable appetite to deepen my understanding of the Bible. Although I had made serious time commitments in studying Scripture—reading it cover to cover twice and rereading numerous sections—I still felt limited in my understanding of God's word because I lacked the interpretive skills and the historical perspective necessary to gain a deeper insight. I began thinking about attending seminary.

Fuller Theological Seminary in Pasadena, California, was having a "prospective student day," and I attended. One of the blessings of that day was the ability to sit in on a class. Like Elizabeth, I was enthralled from the moment the class started, and I sat there wide-eyed for the entire two hours. Immediately, I knew that more formal training in understanding the Scriptures was something I had to do.

It took me several years to finally pursue that dream, due to my inability to figure out how to fit attending school to pursue an advanced degree into my demanding work schedule. However, I received strong confirmation that I had made the right decision once I was accepted at Fuller, decided to pursue a Masters degree in Theology, and started attending classes. Unlike my earlier years in college, where I was often barely doing what was required to earn my degree, I have cherished my time in class, even though it comes with the demands of considerable reading, writing term papers, and studying for midterms and finals.

Jesus says "For where your treasure is, there your heart will be also" (Matthew 6:21). When it comes to furthering our education, I think Elizabeth, the restaurant manager, and I would have reversed that sentence to read, "For where our heart was, there we found our treasure also."

Reflection Point

Key thought

> *One of the primary goals of an education should be to help us align our God-given skills and passions with an appropriate vocation. However, too many of us look at our schooling as a necessary evil required to get a job—or keep one. We often decide on college majors and continuing education classes because of anticipated financial benefits, not because we have a particular passion for the subject matter. Yet, your interest in a particular field of study is an important step in determining the work that God may be leading you toward.*

Questions

1. If you could take a class in *any subject* right now, what would it be?

2. What type of educational opportunity would you be willing to pursue, even if it meant giving up some (or a lot) of your free time?

3. Reflect on your answers to the previous questions and record the class or course of study in the Step 8 section of the journal on page 182.

- -

Step 9: Build a Team of Consultants
Select a mentor, a cheerleader, and a challenger

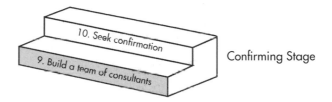

10. Seek confirmation

9. Build a team of consultants

Confirming Stage

In every step of the discernment process, you will wonder whether you are headed in the right direction. It will sometimes be difficult to distinguish between your thoughts and preferences and what God is calling you to do. Your inability to sift out God's thoughts from your own can cause you to be gun shy, and you might retreat into doing nothing.

That's why Steps 9 and 10 are critical to *The Jonah Factor* process. God often speaks to us through other people, especially other believers. Although God could use anyone for this purpose, God is especially effective in communicating to us through those who share our faith and can provide perspective based on that faith and their understanding of how God might be working in our life.

To effectively discern God's direction, you'll need help from others. In addition to having a supportive congregation behind you, it's especially important that you have three specific people on your team of "advisers"—a mentor, a cheerleader, and a challenger.

The mentor

Your mentor is the most important of the three, and there's biblical precedent for this role, as seen in the book of 1 Samuel, where we meet Eli and Samuel.

Eli is an old Jewish high priest; Samuel is a young boy. One night Samuel hears a voice summoning him three different times. It's the older Eli who realizes that it's God's voice, and he instructs Samuel how to respond and to obey what God tells him (Samuel 3:1-10). Samuel understood God's call because he had the help of his trusted mentor. It's much easier for us get a good sense of God's direction with the help of an Eli in our lives.

Your Eli should be someone who has a deeper understanding of Scripture than you do and whose words and actions embody what Jesus says are the two most important commandments: "Love the Lord your God with all your heart and with all your soul and with all your mind and with all your strength" and "Love your neighbor as yourself" (Mark 12:30, 31). In other words, this individual should be a mature Christian whose love of the Lord and concern for you makes her or him a trustworthy sounding board and a conduit through which God's love, encouragement, and wisdom can flow.

Chances are that your first choice of mentor will be a pastor, priest, or other leader at your church or congregation. Indeed, throughout my *Jonah Factor* discernment process I was blessed to have our congregation's now-retired senior pastor, Willis Moerer, as my mentor, a relationship that grew out of my active pursuit of Step 6 when I served on the church council. My involvement in our congregation over the course of almost ten years helped me forge a strong friendship with Wil, giving him unique insights into my weaknesses and strengths that provided him with good markers by which to mentor me. In addition, along the way three other trusted pastors from my congregation, each with different backgrounds and spiritual gifts, stepped in to provide further insights. Again, their interest probably had a lot to do with my involvement in many church ministries and activities, where I became more than a face in the congregation, and they were able to see me in a different role than my family or employer did.

Unfortunately, however, most pastors, priests, and other church leaders are too busy to serve in this valuable, one-on-one role. But if you don't naturally gravitate toward an Eli who could serve as your mentor, your pastor, priest, or lay ministry coordinator might have a recommendation. Some congregations have more formal mentoring programs that can be helpful, and there are a growing number of spiritual directors who are available to help people in the discernment process.

The keys to selecting an effective mentor are choosing someone who:

1. *Is sufficiently trustworthy for you to feel comfortable sharing concerns and exploring "what ifs."* Throughout the discernment process you'll need someone with whom you can share possible ideas or scenarios without someone else learning about them—or laughing at them.

2. *Has deeper knowledge of Scripture than you do.* This individual doesn't have to be a Bible scholar or seminary student. However, he or she should be a faithful reader of God's word, the fruits of which can be seen in his or her life.

3. *Engages in a dedicated prayer life.* A good mentor will pray both alongside you and on your behalf. This individual will be invaluable in helping you decide whether your new sense of mission is coming from you or from God. As I climbed the stairs of discernment, I was continually struck by how frequently my sense of God's purpose for me was shared and thus confirmed by my mentor, Wil. In meetings, he would frequently comment on something—out of the blue—that I was wrestling with or felt God leading me toward. His insights, encouragement, and prayers provided me with increased confidence and conviction.

4. *Is bold enough to tell you when you're off track.* A good mentor is not to be confused with a cheerleader, which we'll discuss next.

The cheerleader

As the name implies, your cheerleader should be someone solidly in your corner during this process. You're not looking at this individual so much as a neutral mentor or adviser; rather you're seeking someone who will cheer you through the valleys you'll encounter in the discernment process. A good cheerleader is an optimist, someone who always sees the glass as half full, at least when it comes to your potential. You'll need that perspective when you hit the tougher stretches, especially during the period when you release one thing (a job, a volunteer activity, a pursuit in school, etc.) and you haven't yet fully embraced the new thing God is calling you to do.

Although family members rarely make good cheerleaders because they are too heavily invested in your success and often fear for your failure, a friend or acquaintance can fill this role well. Preferably this individual will know where you are coming from spiritually and will be prepared to support you even though he or she may occasionally be left scratching his or her head, lacking a complete understanding of what you're going through or trying to do.

I was fortunate to find two cheerleaders, both of them fellow managers at the office where I previously worked. They served in that role at different times. The first cheerleader, Nancy, helped me through the tough days of deciding to and then following through on separating from my employer. She said she increasingly saw in me something very remarkable and godly, comparing me with the fatherly pastor featured on the television show *7th Heaven*. On the mornings after the show aired, she would stop in my office to say, "I saw you on TV last night. I'm telling you, that pastor is you! You come to mind every time that guy says or does anything." Although I didn't discern my next step as going into the pastorate, her insights helped encourage me to go through with my plans to leave my job. I figured that if someone outside of my usual Christian circles saw that in me, there had to be something positive in the path I was pursuing.

The second cheerleader, Dan, took over after I left my position. As I continued to develop the ideas I sensed were to be part of my ministry going forward, his enthusiasm for what I was considering helped me stick with it. In addition, as a manager of my previous firm's Web site, he had key knowledge and insights into how I could expand via the Web the ministry God was more clearly showing me. Dan's cheerleading was critical during the tougher periods after I left my management position, as he continually reminded me of the call that God had placed on my life.

Ironically, both of my cheerleaders left the same firm I did in order to more effectively pursue their own unique vocation, or *vocare* (see chapter 6).

Again, your cheerleader is a person solidly in your corner, urging you on regardless of where your discernment process is leading you. He or she is almost giddy in seeing what you're doing. If your mentor is your neutral adviser, your cheerleader is on the extreme end of the positive scale. For this individual, you can't do wrong.

The challenger

To help counteract the wildly positive perspective of the cheerleader, you'll need to find a challenger. Out of the three people you'll need in Step 7, this person will be the easiest to find. In fact, as you try to discern God's will, several people might try to jump into that role because what you are trying to do is so contradictory to human logic. There will be plenty of people who will either think or tell you that you're crazy.

In spite of the many volunteers who will offer their services for this role, it's important to select only one challenger in whom you'll confide throughout the process.

There are at least two reasons why the challenger is important to the discernment process. First, at the very least, having a more pessimistic individual on your team will prompt you to think things through carefully and not act carelessly on what will most likely be a life-altering decision. Secondly, if you can convince this person that what you're planning to do makes sense, it can be validation that your plans are, indeed, the right ones and not the result of some whim.

Although she didn't know it, I had placed my mother in the role of challenger. Even though she had been extremely supportive of me throughout my college days and during my thirty-year career and had encouraged me to take intelligent risks, I knew that she would be extremely negative toward my seemingly reckless desire to leave my job without knowing what the next step would be. In the months leading up to my decision to leave the job, my mother continually asked the "what if" questions, such as: "As the sole income earner for your family, what if you don't get a comparable salary in what you end up doing?" "What if you're wrong about what you think God is showing you?" "What if you don't have sufficient funds to pay for college for the children?" "What about your plans for retirement; how will you save enough?"

Although I sometimes bristled at her questions, I realized in retrospect that her relentless questioning frequently prompted me to back up and rethink the steps I felt God was showing me. In most cases, that reconsideration brought me to the same conclusions. However, that process made me more confident in the decision I would ultimately make.

Interestingly, once the time came for me to pull the trigger on the decision to leave my job, a remarkable thing happened. My mother concurred that it was the right thing to do. I clearly remember the phone call I made to her prior to submitting the proposal to my firm, eliminating my management position. As I laid out for her what I was planning to do later that week, she said—surprisingly—"You know, this is the right thing for you to do." I believe that as my mother wrestled with God about the decision I was considering, God showed her that it was appropriate. Somehow God had convinced even the most pessimistic person of my advisory team, increasing my confidence in continuing on the path I was now committed to taking.

To effectively discern your next steps and to develop confidence necessary for Step 13, you'll need a strong mentor, cheerleader, and challenger. They represent different ends of the positive/negative spectrum, providing important balance.

Your cheerleader is your incredibly positive fanatic in the bleachers cheering you on. Your challenger is your frowning pessimist who has an eye on your possible failure. And your mentor is the stable center point, providing guidance and alternating between the polar opposites of cheerleader and challenger.

Reflection Point

Key thought

Thoughtfully discerning God's direction is rarely a solitary pursuit. It requires others to point out things we wouldn't see. Up to this point, you haven't sought the advice of others. Now that you're three-quarters of the way through The Jonah Factor *process, it's time to bring in some help. You'll need a mentor, a cheerleader, and a challenger to help guide you, provide feedback, and challenge some of your assumptions.*

Questions

1. Who would be a good mentor to you? Review the key qualities listed on page 119. Pray for God's help in discerning who your mentor might be.

2. Who would make a good cheerleader as you take steps toward the work you think God intends for you? Consider someone who has an optimistic demeanor, understands and supports your spiritual journey, and would be solidly in your corner no matter what your decision is.

3. Who would be a good challenger? Think of someone who might be skeptical about what you're trying to do and wouldn't hesitate to share his or her concerns with you.

4. Once you've selected a mentor, cheerleader, and challenger— and they've agreed to serve in these roles—record their names in the Step 9 section of the journal on page 182.

. . . .

Step 10: Seek Confirmation
Look to insights from family, friends, and a small group

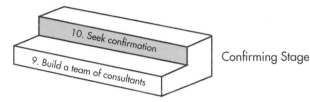

10. Seek confirmation

9. Build a team of consultants

Confirming Stage

Naturally, something as life changing as following God's call requires close collaboration with members of your immediate family. You don't want to just spring it on your spouse and children at the dinner table or on your parents during the Thanksgiving meal. ("Hey honey, I've decided to leave my executive vice president position at the bank and become a sculptor because that's what I think God wants me to do.")

Your family, along with two other groups, will be critical to confirming your direction and then giving you the confidence to take the necessary steps. Share liberally with them what you're thinking, even if you've got just a germ of an idea. Or simply tell them that you're unhappy or unfulfilled in what you're currently doing. Bring them into the thought process at the beginning and make them part of the adventure.

Obviously, if you're married, your spouse should be clued in first. If you're unmarried and your parents are still living, they're an excellent starting point. Then start widening the circle to children, close relatives, close friends, and any Christian small group or Bible study you belong to.

My wife, Lyn, and our two teenage children were incredibly supportive of my decision to follow God's call, in part, I think, because we started talking about it very early in my discernment process. By the time I had formulated a plan, they were behind me to an amazing degree. Lyn knew I had lost the passion for my career and had seen me begin to dread Monday mornings. The kids, too, had seen changes in me. Hannah, sixteen years old at the time, said she noticed how much more animated I became when I talked about the devotions I was writing or the adult education classes I was teaching at church. Our then nineteen-year-old son, Matthew, said he saw a new vigor in me after I had made the decision to leave my corporate position. In fact, he and Hannah later provided profound encouragement to me in their Father's Day cards, in which they told me how proud they were of me as I embarked on this new venture, something every Dad covets.

One caution, however: Be thoughtful about how you approach your children. Certainly, age is a factor here, but emotional and spiritual maturity is equally important. Chances are your decision will have a significant impact on your children, especially if there are likely to be financial consequences. One of Hannah's first questions during discussions about me leaving my job was whether she would still be able to attend her private Christian high school, a place where she had flourished and had so many friends. Try to anticipate your children's questions so you can put any fears to rest early. (Lyn and I had already thought through that issue and decided we would do whatever was necessary to allow Hannah, a junior at the time, to complete her high school education there.)

Friends and relatives can also be helpful in your discernment process, but putting too much emphasis on their input can leave you confused and discouraged, especially if they don't share your faith. Treat their input considerately, but unless an individual is a very close friend or a relative who understands clearly and lovingly what you're trying to do, don't spend too much time soliciting input or put too much emphasis on the advice—often unsolicited—they offer. Instead, rely more on your mentor, cheerleader, and challenger, described in Step 9.

On the other hand, if you're a member of a Bible Study or small group, these fellow Christians can be very helpful in the discernment process. That's especially true if your group is open, loving, and non-judgmental about issues that members bring up.

I've belonged to the same Bible study small group for most of the past fifteen years. During my years of discernment, my small group surrounded me with prayer, love, and encouragement as I took some scary steps of faith. I'm convinced that their prayers—along with those of Lyn, our kids, and others—helped carry me through the more turbulent times of the adventure. Plus, they provided me with insights and confirmation that my direction was appropriate, some of them chiding me for taking so long to come to a conclusion that seemed so obvious to them.

Reflection Point

Key thought
> God places us within communities to provide input, guidance, prayers, and support. Whether through your family, close friends, or your Bible study small group, seek confirmation from others before you commit to the direction you think God is showing you.

Questions
1. Have you shared with any group (family, Bible study, friends) the changes you're considering in the work you do? What has been that group's reaction?

2. When talking with others about what you're considering, do they think it's consistent with talents and abilities you think you have and the direction in which you think you'd like to move?

3. Record, in a few words or phrases, what others in your "confirming group" think you should do in terms of the work to which God may be calling you. Pay particular attention to the input of your immediate family (parents, spouse, children). Record it in the Step 10 section of the journal on page 183.

4. If you are getting negative reactions from your family, friends, or small group, why do you think that is? Do they fully understand what you're trying to do? Do you need to, perhaps, better articulate what you're thinking?

- -

Step 11: Put Out the Fleece
See whether God blesses your initial efforts

12. Be faithful in small things

11. Put out the fleece

Testing Stage

In the book of Judges, Gideon asks for a sign to assure him that God wants him to attack the Midianites. We read in Judges 6:36-38: "Gideon said to God, 'If you will save Israel by my hand as you have promised—look, I will place a wool fleece on the threshing floor. If there is dew only on the fleece and all the ground is dry, then I will know that you will save Israel by my hand, as you said.'"

And that is what happened. Gideon rose early the next day; he squeezed the fleece and wrung out the dew—a bowlful of water.

Perhaps amazed at the result, Gideon repeats the process the next night, with a similar outcome.

You may be surprised to know that we can put God to the test. Somewhere along the road of faith we've concluded that we shouldn't question God. We have this strong sense that a good Christian is someone who salutes and never doubts the words of our Commander in Chief.

Where did we get that impression? It's certainly inconsistent with Scripture, dramatically illustrated in the story of Gideon. Here are other examples:

- The miracles performed by Jesus' disciples, as recorded in the Gospel accounts and the book of Acts, weren't merely intended to heal sick and physically impaired people. They were also proof to the disciples that they were doing God's work, helping them overcome any doubts.
- The ten plagues visited on the Egyptians in Exodus weren't solely to convince Pharaoh to let the Israelites go free. Their

other purpose was to show Moses and the people that God was trustworthy and faithful and that, indeed, Moses was the one anointed to lead God's people from captivity.

• The voice from God at Jesus' baptism, as recorded in Matthew 3:17, wasn't intended to remind Jesus that his Father was pleased with him. It was proof to those who were there that Jesus was, indeed, the promised Messiah.

Throughout Scripture, God offers opportunities for individuals to put out the fleece to help ensure they're headed in the right direction or to confirm what they think God is showing them.

That was true with me, as well. In fact, it was Wil Moerer, my mentor mentioned earlier, who taught me the principle and helped me put it into action. Several years prior to my more radical change in direction, I had talked to him about my sense that God seemed to be nudging me to do something. I was unsure of what it was, but I had the strong feeling that it involved some ministry through our church. I had this vague vision that it would involve speaking to large groups of people. At times, I pictured myself standing in the pulpit of our sanctuary speaking to the congregation.

Wil helped me develop a way of putting out the fleece that would allow God to show us what he had in mind. It led to my becoming church council president for two consecutive terms, a responsibility that presented numerous opportunities for me to speak to large groups at our twenty-five-hundred-member church, many of those opportunities coming from the pulpit.

In my case—and as I've seen happen in other situations—putting out the fleece was a gradual process. Understandably, it wasn't like consulting a Magic 8-Ball®, where you ask a question and turn over the 8-Ball to read a "Yes/No/Maybe" answer that appears in the little window. Rather, it was a process of trying out different things to see which ones clicked.

Wil would present an opportunity (often something like serving on a committee, speaking at a worship service, teaching an adult education class, or participating in a task force). I would then pray about the request, asking God to give me a sense of whether

I should accept the opportunity or not. I would then give Wil my response. Importantly, I turned down more opportunities than I accepted, consistent with how I felt led by God in prayer and in what I saw in my Bible reflection time. I said "no" more often than I said "yes." God clearly showed me which opportunities would be distractions and which ones would help me travel further down the road he was leading me.

One assignment usually led to another, and soon other pastors and members in our congregation were presenting opportunities to me. Again, following prayerful consideration, I declined most of these requests. However, the ones I accepted were incredibly meaningful and provided wonderful opportunities for me to grow in faith and ability. And in looking back at these different "assignments," I saw the path God had carefully placed before me, hidden at the time, but now, in retrospect, crystal clear.

Don't be surprised if you end up putting out more than one fleece, however. The book of Ecclesiastes encourages us to "sow your seed in the morning, and at evening let not your hands be idle, for you do not know which will succeed, whether this or that, or whether both will do equally well" (11:6). As you try to discern what work God intends you to do, you may have to wrestle with two or more competing ideas.

I grappled with several opportunities prior to becoming convinced that I should write this book and begin an outreach to people who were miserable in their work. In addition to looking at a few other corporate positions (just in case God was calling me to a different company), I wrestled with the idea of opening a small shop that sold fine wines.

Following in the footsteps of my father, who years earlier had worked for a wine importing company, I had developed a passion for fine wines, seeing them as the consumable equivalent of a fine painting or sculpture. Over the years I had become knowledgeable about wines and winemaking and had amassed almost five hundred bottles in my collection (many of them since sold off at auction). I dreamed of opening a store that would introduce a growing number of wine enthusiasts to the artistry of fine wines and help them find great wines that had been undiscovered and therefore sold at more reasonable prices.

However, as I progressed through *The Jonah Factor* steps, I realized that my growing obsession with wine was a distraction, one that would derail me from achieving what God had planned. In addition to ongoing prayer and Scripture reading to discern God's direction (Steps 1 and 2), the fleece I put out on this idea was to host a few wine tastings in our home to see whether I had the passion or knowledge to be successful in the business. I quickly discovered that opening a shop and having to deal with fine wines as a full-time occupation exceeded my passions and whatever knowledge I could retain.

In putting out the fleece and reading the results, you'll give God the opportunity to show you things you wouldn't otherwise see. Plus, you'll gain confidence critical to success in Step 13, making it much less frightening than it otherwise might be.

Reflection Point

Key thought

> God expects us to have faith in the journey but doesn't expect it to be blind faith. Along the way, God gives us opportunities to question what we think he is telling us. We're closing in on the climax of The Jonah Factor *process.* Now is a good time to put out the fleece to see if what we're thinking aligns with what God is thinking.

Questions

1. What is most scary or exciting about this concept of "putting out the fleece?"

2. Have you considered—or even tried out—any new responsibilities at your church (from Step 7)? If so, has doing those things confirmed for you the direction you think you need to go in your work? Or has it shown that you need to redirect your efforts into another area?

3. As you've tried some new things (putting out a fleece or two), has anyone validated that you were effective in doing them? If not, why not?

4. Which new activities have most excited you? Which ones have you done extremely well? They could, indeed, be the "fleece" to show you God's blessing or, perhaps, a different direction he wants you to take. Record some brief thoughts in the Step 11 section of the journal on page 183.

· ·

Step 12: Be Faithful in Small Things
Commit to doing the basics

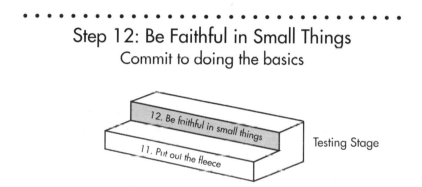

12. Be faithful in small things

11. Put out the fleece

Testing Stage

Prayer, worship, stewardship, and Bible study are the building blocks of developing a close relationship with God and discerning the direction God is leading. None of the other steps in *The Jonah Factor* will be successful without a strong commitment to spending time with God in those four powerful ways. They help prove to him that we are trustworthy.

Jesus talks about this in Luke 16:10 when he says, "Whoever can be trusted with very little can also be trusted with much." God observes how we do the small stuff before we are entrusted with bigger responsibilities and greater opportunities. We can't expect God to grant us those life-changing blessings until we show that we're faithful in doing the basics.

There's another biblical principle at work here, too. Call it the "greater accountability standard." As more and more is revealed to us, and as we receive greater blessing, the Lord's expectations for us also grow. God waits to see what we do with the little stuff as a litmus test for how prepared we are to handle the bigger stuff and whether we'll act appropriately with what we're given.

In Luke 12:48 Jesus gives us deeper insight into this principle, saying, "From everyone who has been given much, much will be demanded; and from the one who has been entrusted with much, much more will be asked." In other words, his expectations increase as we grow in faith and as he prepares to hand us the keys to the kingdom. This can sound like a warning, but it is meant to be seen as a remarkable opportunity. What a privilege it is to be entrusted with greater responsibility and greater opportunities for serving.

Look at how Jesus did this with Peter in Matthew 16. At this point in Jesus' ministry, the disciples have had many opportunities to see him in action. They've witnessed his miracles, listened to his sermons, and watched the life-changing reactions of those who came in contact with him. Finally, there comes a moment of truth. Starting in verse 13 Jesus asks his followers to tell him who people think he is. They respond with a variety of answers: John the Baptist, Elijah, a prophet, etc. Then he asks them a direct question: "Who do *you* say I am?"

Peter is the first to speak, and he acknowledges Jesus as "the Christ, the Son of the living God." In doing so, Peter shows that he grasps the complexities of what he has heard Jesus say and what he has seen him do. His words are a confession of faith. In response, Jesus lays on Peter an incredible responsibility, telling the disciple that he'll lead the church when Jesus departs. In addition, he tells Peter, "I will give you the keys of the kingdom of heaven; whatever you bind on earth will be bound in heaven, and whatever you loose on earth will be loosed in heaven" (Matthew 16:19).

Peter's faithfulness in doing the small things of discipleship prepared him for the big things to which Jesus was now appointing him.

At this point in *The Jonah Factor* process, if you're not getting closer to understanding the plan God has in mind for you, or if you've stopped progressing toward the culmination of that plan, perhaps it's because you're not being faithful in something God has already asked you to do:

- Are you engaged in daily prayer?
- Are you allowing enough quiet time in prayer to hear God's voice and feel his prompting?
- When God encourages you to do something during your prayer time are you faithful in carrying it out?
- Do you attend a worship service at your church at least once a week to praise God in the company of other Christians?
- Do you spend some time each day in the Bible, searching the pages for God's wisdom and direction specifically for you?
- Are you serving God in any capacity, either by volunteering at your church or engaging in a project that carries God's word to others or serves them in God's name?
- Are you a good steward of what God has given you—time, talents, and financial resources?

Each of these is another small step toward knowing God and understanding how God may be leading you. Without engaging in them faithfully, it's doubtful we can be trusted—or prepared for—the big things God has planned for us. Step 13 of *The Jonah Factor* is certainly one of those big things.

Being faithful in small things extends to all that God calls us to during *The Jonah Factor* process. Some of those activities might seem beneath us or a waste of our talents. During my discernment period I took on dozens of simple writing projects—such as letters to the congregation, bulletin inserts, and committee announcements—that, frankly, seemed a waste of my time and the talents I was trying to develop. In retrospect, however, I realize that my successfully completing those assignments gave an increasing number of people the confidence to trust me in more challenging and delicate communications. Plus, they allowed me to more confidently re-enter the writing world from which I'd been absent for almost a decade.

It's being faithful in the small stuff that helps us prepare for the next and final step in *The Jonah Factor* process. And it's a big one!

Reflection Point

Key thought

So far, you've been taking small steps toward your goal. If you've committed yourself to doing them thoughtfully and completely, you've probably seen God's faithfulness at work. Hopefully you've sensed God building you up, confirming certain ideas, and providing the revelation necessary for you to make a leap of faith toward the joyful work God is calling you to do. Before you proceed to the final step, however, make sure you haven't overlooked any steps or gone through them too quickly. In addition, ask yourself whether you've been faithful in doing the smaller things necessary for building you up to take the next big step.

Questions

1. How are your prayer time and Scripture time going? Have you been consistent? Why or why not?

2. How have you thoughtfully tried to examine your talents and passions and evaluated whether you're able to use them in your current job?

3. Have you joined a congregation and gotten involved in some ministry or service that allows you to try out those talents and determine if you would have a long-term passion for doing that kind of work?

4. How have you been engaged in learning new information and skills that would be appropriate in the work you'd like to do?

5. Who makes up your team of three consultants?

6. How have family, friends, or others and the activities you have chosen to do confirmed the direction God is leading you?

7. How have you been faithful in carrying out what you've perhaps felt were less significant activities in serving God, yet are ones that lead toward the work you ultimately seek?

8. As you look back at everything you've done in the twelve steps you've engaged in so far, is there one job, activity, or field of study that continues to stand out as one you should pursue? Write that down in the Step 12 section of the journal on page 184.

. . . .

Step 13: Take the Leap of Faith
It will be easier than you think

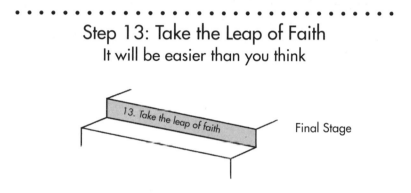

Final Stage

In *The Return of the King*, the last installment of *The Lord of the Rings* movie trilogy, hobbits Frodo and Sam work their way up to and inside of Mount Doom to destroy the ring. The freedom of Middle Earth depends on their success.

Sam and Frodo overcome a myriad of obstacles, each one another step toward fulfilling their mission as they make their way across the countryside and then up the mountain. However, there comes a point where the steps toward their goal literally run out, and they're required to take a great leap of faith to complete the mission. As the mountain crumbles around them, they gather up their courage and make that leap.

That's what it's like when we're following God's leading.

Most of the time during *The Jonah Factor* process, we're taking small steps toward the goal. Our confidence builds as we learn to trust God and we see God's faithfulness in the small risks we're taking, even though we occasionally wonder where the journey is headed. At some point—and perhaps several along the way—we have to jump and trust that God will catch us.

That image of stepping into a void and being caught was a vivid one for me—and one that frequently punctuated my prayer time as I wrestled with God's call for me to take a leap of faith. Reflecting my concern about the unknowns in the decision I was being asked to make, I often pictured myself at the edge of a chasm, looking down into it, unable to see anything below. I was staring into darkness. I could hear God calling me to leap, but I was frozen on the ledge. Each time I refused to jump. For months that image returned during times of quiet prayer.

One day, during a particularly vivid encounter with God in prayer, I finally gathered my courage and imagined myself jumping into the void. And the strangest thing happened: Almost immediately I felt someone catch me and guide me to a safe landing, first on a ledge and then on solid ground. The experience felt incredibly real. And, strangely, I didn't recognize the place where I had landed. All I knew was that it looked completely different than the place from which I had jumped.

As mentioned previously, building up to this step will seem scary at first. As you anticipate what could be dramatic changes resulting from a new job or direction, your mind may start racing, with images of doom or at the very least the sacrifices you think you may have to make to fulfill the destiny that God has in mind for you. Don't worry about that right now. God is incredibly faithful.

God tells Jeremiah, "Blessed is the man who trusts in the LORD, whose confidence is in him" (Jeremiah 17:7). That's echoed in Hebrews 10:35-36, "So do not throw away your confidence; it will be richly rewarded. You need to persevere so that when you have done the will of God, you will receive what he has promised."

The importance of perseverance in following through on this step is best summed up in a quote attributed to the late U. N. Secretary General Dag Hammarskjöld: "There is a point at which everything becomes simple and there is no longer any question of choice, because all you have staked will be lost if you look back. Life's point of no return."

The intent of *The Jonah Factor* is to guide you to that point of no return. The previous twelve steps are intended to provide you with insights into God's plan for you, to compel you into taking an action that you wouldn't otherwise take. If you have thoughtfully and prayerfully climbed the previous steps, you will be convinced that this leap is the right thing to do. You'll realize that there's no turning back.

In many ways, reaching Step 13 can be compared to graduating from college. During the years leading up to graduation we take small steps in trying to discern direction. Early on, we may have had no idea of what to major in or what career would be most appropriate, so we rely on the stepping stones of our general education classes to shine some light on areas in which we have an aptitude. We also discover what we're not so good at. Many of us change majors during this time as we learn more about ourselves, our vocational passions, and our strengths and weaknesses. As we narrow in on an appropriate major, things become clearer. Our discernment grows as we keep going up the stairway. Some of us engage in internships or summer jobs attempting to see how much we'd enjoy those "real world" jobs that our education is preparing us for. We make adjustments based on those observations.

However, the time eventually comes for us to step onto the ledge and graduate. At that point we have to take a leap of faith that our education, training, internships, and other research has prepared us to jump into the real world, trusting that we are ready.

Some graduates never make the leap successfully. They're stranded on the ledge of life, unwilling to take the step that will change everything. Some decide to stay in school, treading water under the auspices of furthering their education (not to be confused with someone purposefully going for an advanced degree). Others leave college never going into the field for which they've studied, choosing safer, less demanding occupations.

Regardless of how close you've come toward fulfilling what God created you to do, there will come a point at which you'll have to do a swan dive into the chasm, trusting God for your safety. If you have been faithful, thoughtful, and discerning throughout the other twelve steps of *The Jonah Factor*, you will land safely. You may not end up where you had expected, and that's probably a good thing. God's plans for us are usually much bigger than the plans we dream up for ourselves.

Remember the promise in Jeremiah 29:11, when God says, "'For I know the plans I have for you,' declares the LORD, 'plans to prosper you and not to harm you, plans to give you hope and a future.'"

Knowing exactly when to take the leap of faith is probably the most difficult aspect of this final step. That's because this is the collision point of human logic and God's will. Making the significant life change that God intends for us, especially one that seems risky financially or socially, will seem contradictory to a fulfilling life. After all, chances are that we've worked hard to get to where we are. Jumping into the chasm will seem like we're throwing everything away.

However, that's an incorrect perception because God never wastes anything.

God is the ultimate recycler. Regardless of what God is calling you to do—whether it's a different job, field of study, ministry, or volunteer activity—he will use the skills, talents, and abilities you've developed over your lifetime so far. Look at what God does with the rainwater that spills off your roof. It seems like a waste to have a precious resource like water channeled into a series of gutters and drainage ditches that ultimately carry it back out to sea. However, along the way that water supplies life to streams and lakes and rivers, all part of God's plan. Nothing gets wasted.

I've seen that in the almost two years since I took my leap of faith. Just about every skill that I've worked hard to develop in my half century of life has been necessary to make the shift from corporate wonk to writer, speaker, and small business owner. In fact, today I'm using a broader range of talents and abilities than at any other time in my life.

There's a reason why Step 13 is called the "leap of faith." Taking it will require considerable trust in God. And, for a while, you might find yourself frozen on the edge, unable to jump. Chapter

12 deals with some of the most common reasons for our reluctance to take the leap.

However, as you prepare to jump off the ledge, hang onto the powerful promise of Proverbs 16:3: "Commit to the LORD whatever you do, and your plans will succeed."

Reflection Point

Key thought

> *Leaps of faith can be scary, even when we've done everything possible to build up to them. We may never feel completely comfortable in making the leap, but that's where faith comes in. If you've been thoughtful in each step of The Jonah Factor process, you've probably developed greater confidence in making the leap into what God is calling you to. At this point, you can either stay safely on the edge of the precipice (missing out on the adventure God has planned for you) or you can gather up your courage and swan dive into the void. God will help you finish what you and God have started together. It's time to leap.*

Questions

1. What concerns you most about taking a leap of faith?

2. Are you reluctant to take that leap? If so, why?
    - ❑ Possible financial sacrifices
    - ❑ Fear of failure
    - ❑ Discomfort with change
    - ❑ Unsure of whether God is, indeed, calling you to make this change
    - ❑ Something else

3. If you're stuck and unable to commit to taking the leap of faith, review what you've entered in the different sections of the journal starting on page 178. Remind yourself of what

God has revealed to you so far and look for consistency in those steps. If there are glaring inconsistencies (such as too many different ideas that don't lead logically to the direction in which you should now move), revisit the steps, lingering especially on Steps 1 and 2.

4. If you're still stuck, read on. I'll share some more insights into *The Jonah Factor* process. And perhaps you'll see yourself in some of the pages that follow.

CHAPTER EIGHT

Leap-of-Faith Fears

Energy and persistence conquer all things.

—*Benjamin Franklin*

IF YOU FOLLOW EACH OF THE STEPS IN *THE JONAH FACTOR* PROCESS, YOU WILL BE IN A POSITION TO TAKE STEP 13 (THE LEAP OF FAITH). If you have prepared well by following Steps 1 through 12, you may find Step 13 to be the easiest one of all. But second thoughts and mild to serious concerns will crop up for even the most confident among us. That's natural. After all, by allowing God this amount of control over your life you're doing something very abnormal for humans. The decision to take this leap of faith will be contrary to almost everything you've been taught from an early age.

Once you've committed to taking that leap of faith, there may be times when you wake up at 2 A.M. in a cold sweat, asking yourself,

"What the heck am I doing?" Most of your concerns will probably fit into one of the following categories.

Fear #1: Fear of Financial Loss

Few of us have the financial resources to immediately make a change that could lower or temporarily eliminate our income. Trusting God is one thing, but each of us has responsibilities to ourselves, to our families, and to our mortgage holders. My most frequent financial concerns after committing to the leap of faith had to do with covering college costs for our two teenagers, one who was already in college and the other quickly approaching that major "cha-ching" point. I found great encouragement in prayer, and I also took a practical approach, going back to the budget I had sketched out and reminding myself of what resources we had and how each dollar had come from God to begin with.

Don't minimize any financial impact your leap of faith might have. Conversely, don't place too much emphasis on your finances. This is a journey of faith, after all, and we know that a God who cares even about the flowers of the field or the birds of the air (Matthew 6:25-34) is concerned about your well-being.

Frankly, you might not be able to take the leap of faith as soon as you'd like. That's why there's no exact timeline for *The Jonah Factor*. For some people, the process leading up to Step 13 might take six months. For others, however, getting there might require a few years as you discern God's plan and get your financial house in order. I have several friends who are unable to take the leap of faith they're being called to until they pay down substantial debt. In the meantime, they're preparing for it.

Financial issues are important, but they shouldn't be show stoppers. Plus, if we're humbly seeking God's will, we have to give God some room to maneuver, especially when it comes to our lifestyle.

Many of us want God to operate according to our parameters, especially in the financial realm. We box God in by saying, "Please show me what you want me to do with my life, but let me keep the comfortable lifestyle I have." We limit God's ability to lead us in the right direction because we constrain God with our wants.

As you'll see in chapter 13, my family and I were required to make lifestyle sacrifices, most of them surrounding an expensive house that we loved. Once we walked away from that particular trap, God opened up unimaginable doorways and provided new direction. Selling our house and downsizing our lifestyle provided financial blessings far beyond what I had anticipated. It dramatically lowered our monthly expenses (mortgage payments decreased, utility bills were cut in half, insurance costs went down dramatically, and other cost-of-living expenses saw significant cuts). Taking out some of the equity we had built up over the years provided us with the financial life raft to make it to the shores that God led us to.

If you're struggling with the financial downside of taking the leap of faith, sit down with a financial adviser, preferably one who shares your faith. Tell them what you're trying to do and get their advice about the best ways to proceed financially. It might make sense to pay them by the hour to have them do a financial inventory of your assets and liabilities. If you don't have an adviser, interview a few. Choose one who seems to have the best understanding of what you're trying to do and your motivation for doing it. Avoid anyone who listens for a couple of minutes and then tries to sell you a whole range of products, most of which will generate commissions or incentives.

In my more than ten years in the mutual fund business, I've met several hundred financial advisers across the United States. I've learned that you can quickly identify the best ones by how thoughtfully they listen and how purposefully they try to determine their clients' goals in life before they try to provide any solutions.

However, don't use the adviser as a sounding board for whether you should take the leap of faith. Rather, have the adviser take a look at your financial situation and advise you on *how* you'll be able to do what God is calling you to. Be especially open to lifestyle changes the adviser might recommend. Remember, you're looking for a way to do what God is calling you to do and should be prepared to make sacrifices to make it possible.

Don't constrain God with the creature comforts and luxuries you feel you can't do without. Be willing to let go of whatever isn't necessary to finding the joy God intends for your work.

Fear #2: Concern about What Others Might Say

The Jonah Factor concept contradicts the wisdom of the world. Your decision to follow God's leading will drive a few people crazy, especially some close friends and family members. Even fellow believers might question the leap of faith you've decided to take, and they may scare you into doubting yourself.

Realize, however, that you are following a very biblical principle as you take these 13 Steps. That is, you are trying to kill off the "old self." Ephesians 4:22-23 speaks to that when it says, "You were taught, with regard to your former way of life, to put off your old self, which is being corrupted by its deceitful desires; to be made new in the attitude of your minds; and to put on the new self, created to be like God in true righteousness and holiness."

Volumes have been written about the meaning of those verses, but here's how we can apply them to our pursuit of joyful and God-ordained work and other activities. Romans 5 tells us to put the "old Adam" to death. Adam, the first human, represents our human nature, which we continually struggle against in trying to carry out God's will. It's the selfish, I-want-to-do-things-my-way mentality that's embedded in our human nature, not our spiritual one. When Jesus was put to death, his life as an "Adam" ended. He died to that old life. When he rose from the dead, he unveiled a new way of life for all of us, a life in the Spirit. *The Jonah Factor* is aimed at directing you toward that life in the Spirit.

Even as Christians, we tend to want to live like the "old Adam," which chooses security through physical means (money, possessions, ego, etc.). But when we are in relationship with Jesus Christ, the "new Adam," our focus can be on the spiritual dimension of our lives. We can be free to live in new ways. To rely on the physical, as many of us do, gets in the way of an intimate relationship with our Lord. In other words, it brings sin. To overcome the pull of the physical, the Apostle Paul in Romans 6 makes a radical statement: we need to "crucify" ourselves with Christ. He says, "For we know that our old self was crucified with (Jesus) so that the body of sin might be done away with, that we should no longer be slaves to sin—because anyone who has died has been freed from sin."

Bible lessons aside, by seeking the wrong things in the work we do (money, prestige, perks) instead of the right ones (fulfillment of God's purpose, a life pleasing to God, and alignment with values consistent with what God is calling us to do), we're living in the flesh instead of the Spirit. Unfortunately, that's how most of us live, even longtime Christians. It's so easy for us to get our priorities wrong. This includes clinging to material possessions for security. When that is such a prevalent attitude in our culture, you can expect people to question what you are doing. And that's why you may get flack when you tell others about your anticipated leap of faith.

On another level, others may question why you are walking away from something that seems to fit your abilities, or which looks like the logical culmination of a career track. In this case, you will simply have to expect that some people will not understand. If you are confident in the direction God is leading you, those opinions simply won't matter.

That's why the first two steps in *The Jonah Factor* process are so important. They will ground you in faith and in hearing God's voice. In the process, you'll crucify yourself with Jesus in a wonderful way. You'll develop a deeper, more intimate relationship with God, whose voice will then be loud enough to drown out the naysayers who will inevitably raise their voices as you tell others what you intend to do.

In my experience, the people most skeptical about my leap of faith were at the firm I was leaving. In announcing my departure, I was open about the important role my faith had in my decision. I was living in the Spirit, and it gave me a boldness I didn't think possible. I candidly told many of my coworkers that I felt God was leading me in a different direction. A few questioned my sanity (really!) while some others rolled their eyes. Most difficult for people—even believers—to understand was that I was leaving a great job without knowing what I would do next. They had difficulty understanding how the sole income earner for a family of four could jeopardize his and his family's future by simply trusting that God would see him through.

That's why Steps 9 and 10 are also so important. By building a core of people who have a deeper understanding of the call of God in your life and how that is affecting your choices, and you'll be less apt to doubt your decision based on the input of others around you. If you rely on the people you've selected for the "confirming" stage of *The Jonah Factor,* you'll be much less affected by the cynicism of others.

Fear #3: Second Thoughts (Also Known As "Cold Feet")

The Jonah Factor can involve a long haul, even once you've taken the leap of faith. There will be times when you'll want to change the plan, especially if you're in the midst of an interim period where nothing seems to be happening. You'll doubt your decision, questioning whether God was indeed directing you this way.

That happened several times after I had stepped off the ledge in Step 13, mostly in the form of being contacted for other corporate opportunities. Frankly, I strongly considered one of those positions. It came at a weak moment, as I looked at our dwindling finances and realized that both of the business opportunities I felt God was calling me to would take many months—perhaps years—to generate sufficient income. In addition, I sometimes strayed onto companies' Web sites to check their open positions, a path clearly opposed to the one onto which I felt God leading me.

However, Dan, one of my Step 9 cheerleaders, stepped in at a critical juncture as I shared with him what I was considering. He reminded me of the broader purpose of what God was trying to do in and through my life. I also re-engaged more deeply in Steps 1 and 2 during that period. I was reminded of God's provision and encouraged to stick with the plan through a verse I came across in Ephesians: "Now to him who is able to do immeasurably more than all we ask or imagine, according to his power that is at work within us" (3:20). I was reminded that God's power was more than ample in helping me follow through on what we had set out to do together.

Fear #4: Not Being Completely Convinced

To effectively take the leap of faith, you've got to be convinced that you're doing the right thing. Remember, you're not doing this based on some whim, dissatisfaction at work, or because you're bored. You're doing this because you are convinced that this pursuit is exactly what God wants you to do. You're tired of being a Jonah, of running away from God's call. You're ready to be released from the belly of the big fish.

If you're having serious doubts about taking the leap of faith, revisit the other twelve steps. This will do two things. First, it will show you whether you've skipped any steps or haven't gotten the confirmation along the way to move to the next level. You might realize that you've rushed certain steps or even stages. Secondly, if you've followed the process properly, it will confirm that you're doing the right thing. For example, revisiting Step 7 (pursue opportunities at your church or congregation) might remind you of the good experiences you had in trying out new things and confirm for you that your leap of faith is appropriate and possible. There are countless other fears and phobias that might creep into your thinking. The Bible reminds us that God's opponent, Satan, will work hard to prevent you from achieving that which God has planned for you. He is the great deceiver, the one who "leads the whole world astray" (Revelation 12:9). Satan knows us better than we realize, and he continually plays on our fears to throw us off course.

Don't be dissuaded by whatever fears crop up as you continue up *The Jonah Factor* stairway. Continue to be purposeful in your discernment, and once you're convinced that your leap of faith is appropriate, pray that God's Spirit will stop anything, including Satan, from talking you out of it.

Be aware also of what John Eldridge, in his book *Wild at Heart*, calls "the traitor within": our weak flesh that consistently wants to take the easy way out and smother what the Holy Spirit beckons us to do.

Reflection Point

Key thought

> *Leaping into the void requires courage, even when you've strapped on a parachute. Your heart may say "Go ahead and jump," but your mind is screaming, "Hey, we could get killed doing this!" There are different fears that keep us frozen at the edge. If you recognize the culprit that's keeping you from embracing the adventure ahead, there's a good chance you'll finally be able to take that step in faith.*

Questions

1. Which of the fears listed in this chapter is holding you back?
   - ❏ Fear #1: Fear of financial loss
   - ❏ Fear #2: Concern about what others might say
   - ❏ Fear #3: Second thoughts
   - ❏ Fear #4: Not being completely convinced

   What other fears may be holding you back?

2. Think about the worst thing that would happen if you failed in your attempt to move into the more rewarding work you've identified in the journal starting on page 178. How likely is your worst-case scenario?

3. How would your life still be rewarding if your worst-case scenario came about in a partial way?

4. What if you finally found the job of a lifetime, one that would bring your life considerable joy and purpose? What would you be willing to sacrifice in other areas of your life to make this happen?

Part Five

· · · · · · · · · · · · ·

Encouragements

I just needed to turn my life over

to whoever came up with redwood trees.

—*Anne Lamott in* Plan B: Further Thoughts on Faith

The way to succeed is never quit.

That's it. But be really humble about it.

—*Alex Haley*

CHAPTER NINE

Countless
Blessings

Jesus looked at them and said,

"With man this is impossible, but not with God;

all things are possible with God."

—Mark 10:27

Earlier I gave some examples of how God provided encouragement as I progressed through *The Jonah Factor* steps. There were countless others. While I was engaged in each of the 13 Steps, God's power and faithfulness were displayed to me in awesome ways, providing visible proof that I was following God's leading.

In Malachi, God gives us a hint of the blessings that get poured upon those who are faithful. God says, "Test me in this . . . and see if I will not throw open the floodgates of heaven and pour out so much blessing that you will not have room enough for it" (3:10).

My family and I were recipients of countless blessings that I believe were activated by my leap of faith.

Let me give you just an overview of those blessings. Most of them are probably unique to my adventure in faith. However, trust that God has similar and equally wonderful blessings in store for you as you prepare for a leap of faith.

As I indicated in the introduction, I had known for a long time that God was prompting me to do something different with my life. It started as gentle whispers, literally, and grew louder as I, like Jonah, resisted God's call. I was in my forties, prime time for that male diversion called the "midlife crisis." In fact, for many years I simply wrote off these whispers as indicative of that life stage, minus the Porsche. Just as Jonah was comfortably ensconced in his role as a prophet in the northern kingdom of Israel during the early part of his life, I was in a job and a lifestyle I saw no reason to give up.

A Growing Faith

The years during which I wrestled with this call were also a time of intense growth in my faith. I set out to study the Bible cover to cover, made a greater commitment to daily prayer, and my family and I began attending worship services at our church each week. An inscription on a new light switch plate we installed near the front door announced: "As for me and my house, we will serve the Lord" (Joshua 24:15). And, indeed, that was our goal.

In my prayer, worship, and Bible study time, my feelings increasingly were transformed into convictions. However, instead of exciting me, they brought confusion and fear. After all, at that point I was almost thirty years into a lucrative career, and I had assumed I would retire from a corporate position once I had put enough money away to escape from the daily pressures and the long commute.

However, the once-quiet voice grew louder, and as I more purposefully sought out God's will for my life—the steps of which became *The Jonah Factor*—my fears subsided. They were replaced by an increasing confidence.

Two things, both of which I initially found in the Bible, helped me turn the corner and gain the conviction to move ahead. The first, as mentioned previously, was my stumbling across Revelation 21:21, in which Jesus says, "Behold, I make all things new." Those words jumped out at me when I glanced at that page because they answered a question I had been struggling with: In my discontent, what was God trying to tell me? I found the answer in that verse. God was trying to do something completely new in my life. Strangely, in the two weeks following this discovery, that verse popped up several more times in different situations. Our church bulletin normally runs an inspirational verse each Sunday and that week the verse was—you guessed it—"Behold, I make all things new." The following week I was wrapping up a phone conversation with our associate pastor, Tim Delkeskamp, when he closed the call with, out of the blue: "Remember, Ed, 'Behold I make all things new.'"

Another subtle encouragement to take a step in faith was delivered in a sermon by Pastor Tim a few weeks later. The theme was about how God calls people to take leaps of faith, and the sermon centered on Genesis 12:1, in which God calls Abram (God later renames him Abraham) to "Leave your country, your people, and your father's household and go to the land I will show you." God was asking Abraham to leave the past behind and travel to a destination that he hadn't yet revealed.

As I pondered that verse and the rest of the chapter, it answered for me the question that most gripped me with fear: Although I knew I was being called to do something different, what was it that I was supposed to do? The sermon and the accompanying Scripture seemed to be saying that God wouldn't show me the next steps until I, like Abraham, trusted God and took the required leap of faith.

A Plan Emerges

This corresponded with the "chasm" vision I mentioned earlier. The unseen bottom of the abyss represented the destination God planned for me. As that image repeatedly came to mind, I developed the confidence to trust God in the risks I was about to take.

This time period was punctuated with numerous family roundtable discussions over dinner. I shared with Lyn and the kids my dissatisfaction with the job and the new direction I was sensing. We prayed together for God's guidance. In my solitary prayer time I asked God to help them understand that I wasn't crazy. Over time, Lyn and the kids understood my dissatisfaction with my current position and that what I was hoping to do would involve a leap of faith for all of us. We committed our plans to God, asking that God take care of us, although we understood God might not do so in the way we had hoped.

Trusting God was one thing. But leave it to our then sixteen-year-old daughter, Hannah, always the most acerbic of the family, to quip one day: "But Dad, don't you think you should have a backup plan?"

Scripture describes many situations in which God encourages people to go somewhere else. Jonah was ordered to go to Nineveh; Abraham was told to travel to an unidentified land. Paul was given a vision to share the gospel among the Gentiles. God's call to me was to leave my position. In fact, I felt God calling me from my profession to do something completely different. But how would I do that, especially since our savings would have only kept us afloat for several months?

God had a plan.

A number of managers and I were considering a restructuring of our department to meet new business needs, the kind of reshuffling that most corporations engage in every few years. Increasingly, I felt compelled to propose an option that would eliminate my position. As I pursued the idea, a proposal unfolded almost naturally. It was one in which all of my responsibilities could be given to others on my staff. My hope was that, by making my job elimination part of a restructuring, the company would provide me with a short-term severance package. It would also allow me to collect unemployment insurance while I sorted things out, which included looking for another position elsewhere. That combination would end up providing the financial life raft we needed.

My proposal was accepted almost immediately, leading me to believe that discussions had already been underway about eliminating my management level as part of a more comprehensive restructuring the company was undertaking. In spite of that, I believe my submitting the proposal was a critical step in showing my trust in God and was now ready to go on whatever adventure God had planned.

Why Not Sell the House?

Before the dust had even settled from my job elimination announcement, Lyn made an astonishing suggestion: Why not sell our house and downsize to a smaller home, taking out some of the equity that had built up during the white-hot real estate market in our area over the previous three years? Without knowing it, she was putting out the fleece of *The Jonah Factor*'s Step 11.

I was resistant at first. My reaction was indicative of how much ego I had wrapped up in that house. You see, we lived in our dream home. Purchased only three years previously, this house epitomized for us the good life in Southern California. The home was not only spacious and comfortable; it fed my ego by announcing to everyone who visited that I was successful. I was incredibly reluctant to sell something into which I had wrapped so much of my self worth.

Lyn had no such misconceptions about the house, however. To her this structure represented another opportunity to pump some more air into our financial life raft. She persisted, and I finally relented.

I wasn't willing to give in that easily, however. I had a scheme that would both satisfy Lyn (or at least mollify her) and keep us in my dream house. We would list it at a price far above what I thought the market would bear. Although we would be selling in a very hot real estate market, I would ratchet the asking price above what I thought anyone would be willing to pay. My justification was that a higher selling price would provide that much more of a cushion.

Debra, a friend of ours who is a real estate agent, understood what we were trying to do (although she didn't realize my ulterior motive). She offered to list our house and help us find a more modest home. However, even she was shocked when I told her the price I wanted for the house. Although the real estate market in our area was very active at the time, the price at which I wanted to list the house was almost 10 percent above even the most generous appraisal. As a Christian, though, she understood what we were trying to do, and she agreed to take it on.

We signed the papers on a Friday night, meaning our listing wouldn't appear in the Multiple Listing Service (a real estate agent's Bible of housing inventory in the area) until that following Monday. To take advantage of the market and get a leg up on other agents, Debra decided to host an open house that Sunday.

The door was supposed to open at 1 P.M. At ten minutes before the hour a family rang the doorbell and made an offer on the house—slightly ABOVE our asking price. Later we learned that the buyers were acquaintances of one of our neighbors and had been interested for years in moving into our neighborhood.

Strangely, only a few weeks before the buyers had made the offer, the wife had commented to our neighbor that she had a dream about a house on our small cul-de-sac coming onto the market and that they had bought it. I'm not a big believer in modern-day visions and dreams, but all of these "coincidences" began to convince even a skeptic like me.

Learning Humility

God's sense of humor—and the opportunity to teach me some humility—came through in our transition to a new home. I had always steadfastly refused to consider living in a townhome because I valued the greater privacy and quiet that most single family homes afford.

Throughout our twenty-five-year marriage and our four homes, we had lived in single family houses. This time, however, God steered us toward a townhome, the price of which was being reduced.

God's provision sometimes has a cost, and we think, initially, that we're giving up something substantial. Over time, however, we learn that the sacrifice wasn't all that significant. In fact, it turns into a blessing. Ultimately, I understood our new townhome to be that blessing as we traded in a home at which gardening and maintenance took up too much valuable weekend time for one in which the backyard is no more than a patio, allowing me to concentrate on the work that God is calling me to do and significantly reducing the costs of home ownership.

Much like the immediate and stunning sale of our home and the purchase of the new one, our lives during this time were a buzz of activity. Everything happened simultaneously. Both my last day on the job and the closings on both houses occurred on the same day, which could have made this a particularly stressful time. Yet we had a remarkable peace in the midst of this storm. All of the elements involved in ending a career, selling a house, and buying another house came together amazingly well, proving to us once again that God is incredibly faithful. We saw that as further confirmation that our leap of faith was the right one.

The amazing adventure continued as Lyn discerned the need to return to full-time employment outside the home after fifteen years as a stay-at-home mom, homemaker, and volunteer for several important ministries. Obviously, the income would help us significantly. Plus, a full-time job would allow us access to a company-sponsored health care plan, for which we were now paying more than $1,000 a month.

Lyn had learned of an employment opportunity at a nearby university, her alma mater, ironically. She jumped at the chance to see whether she was still "employable." Given the significant responsibilities of this position and the expertise required, getting the job was a stretch since Lyn had been out of the workforce for so long. Once again, however, God's provision became apparent. Lyn interviewed for the position on a Friday and then again on the following

Monday. She was hired immediately and asked to start the next day. Our financial life raft was about to get another infusion of air.

Although I had completed all 13 Steps of *The Jonah Factor*, I was really only halfway through the discernment process, because I still didn't know exactly what God was calling me to do. So far, all I had done was leave a job and move into a smaller home.

To discern exactly what God was calling me to do, I re-employed all 13 Steps of *The Jonah Factor* process, doing so even more purposefully, because I now was able to set aside more time each day. God continued to guide us in the adventure that lay before us, which increasingly became clear.

A Peek at the Promised Land

The land that God showed me was a writing and speaking ministry to share my experiences and use the talents I had sharpened earlier while engaged in *The Jonah Factor* steps.

I applied to and was accepted at Fuller Theological Seminary, furthering my hopes of discerning whether God wanted me to deepen my insights into Scripture and my faith by obtaining a Masters degree in Theology. I set time aside almost each day to write *The Jonah Factor*. And I further developed the *Digging Deeper* daily devotions publication I had been producing, to determine whether I could turn these popular writings into a business or possibly collect them into a book.

In John 20:30 we get a sense of the awesome number of miracles Jesus must have performed. We read that "Jesus did many other miraculous signs in the presence of the disciples, which are not recorded in this book." These were *in addition* to those recorded in the Gospel accounts. My story is similar in that I have been an eyewitness to countless miracles—truly happenings beyond my power or plans—that blessed us during this "adventure." They far exceed what I have described in this chapter.

Since "the adventure" began, not a month has gone by that we haven't seen some kind of unexpected blessing—often of the financial kind—that allows us to stay afloat as I build the ministry

God has given me. More importantly, each blessing has allowed us to take further steps in faith.

It is interesting how often God chose financial blessings as a way of confirming those steps, because my greatest concerns were regarding money. During the early part of the adventure, we received a number of unexpected checks, some of them refunds or corrections in our favor on the real estate transactions we had conducted earlier. They were blessings I hadn't planned into our budget. Also, as I tried to discern whether God was calling me to a different corporate position, I was able to draw from unemployment insurance for several months. (In California and other states, those who collect unemployment must be involved in a job search, something I did during those six months to determine whether God was calling me to a different position elsewhere.)

Other unanticipated financial blessings came in the form of writing assignments, love offerings from one of the congregations that was subscribing to *Digging Deeper*, and the opportunity to consult on a research study at a nearby university, all of which helped keep us afloat as I wrote this book.

As time progressed, however, the greatest financial blessings came in the form of lower expenses, partly due to our downsizing, mentioned earlier. God also assisted in that effort by providing some unanticipated expense reductions, such as a doubling of the scholarship my daughter, Hannah, received for her senior year at the private Christian high school she had attended.

Much like John recorded in his Gospel account (see also 21:25), I started losing track of the many ways in which God miraculously blessed us in our endeavor.

My story is simple in one sense. I've had to trust God financially, and God has continued to bless me and my family in ways that both confirmed my leap-of-faith decision and allowed me to do what I have been called to do.

Like manna in the desert, God met our needs as we worked our way toward the new land God was now showing us.

Part Six

· · · · · · · · · · · · · ·

Tailoring
The Jonah Factor

If you enjoy what you do,

you will never work another day in your life.

—*Confucius*

Don't ask yourself what the world needs.

Ask yourself what makes you come alive,

and go do that, because what the world needs

is people who have come alive.

—*Gil Bailie*

CHAPTER TEN

For the Less Traditional Career

To finish the moment,

to find the journey's end in every step of the road,

to live the greatest number of good hours, is wisdom.

—*Ralph Waldo Emerson*

THROUGHOUT MOST OF THIS BOOK WE'VE LOOKED AT HOW *THE JONAH FACTOR* CAN BE APPLIED TO CAREERS OR OCCUPATIONS. But what about those of us who are in a different stage of life or whose time is spent on less traditional pursuits, such as retirement or as full-time students? And what about someone who is already serving God through full-time ministry?

The Jonah Factor can be helpful in perceiving God's prompting regardless of occupation, pursuit, or life stage. Each of the 13

Steps is appropriate, but some of the steps take on different levels of importance.

For the Stay-at-Home Parent

Frankly, there is no greater challenge—or reward—than being a stay-at-home mom or dad. It is one of the toughest jobs in the world, especially when children are under five years old. It's uniquely demanding work that requires stamina, quick thinking, and a generous dose of love and grace.

Stay-at-home parenting is similar to other jobs, however, in that there are stages. During the pre-school stage, caring for children requires almost twenty-four-hour attention, and there's little that the homebound mom or dad can do outside the home, except to escape for some R&R every so often when they're relieved by the other parent. Once children enter school, there are opportunities for the stay-at-home parent to look for some part-time opportunities, perhaps volunteer activities or starting a very small business.

My wife, Lyn, stopped working outside the home a couple of years after our second child, Hannah, was born. Although we had some lean years initially, it was an excellent decision, one that had positive effects for years to come. Having her stay at home brought a peace and joy to our home that had eluded us.

Initially, Lyn was a full-time mom with no outside activities. However, as our children progressed in elementary school, she became involved in an increasing number of volunteer activities while they were at school, culminating in a leadership position at a local chapter of an international group called Bible Study Fellowship. As the kids continued to grow up, Lyn transitioned into her own small business, a Mary Kay Cosmetics consultancy. All of these outside activities gave her considerable flexibility in hours, allowing her to be at home when the children were out of school, something a more rigid job wouldn't have allowed.

This process required significant discernment. With the multitude of volunteer and small business opportunities available, Lyn spent considerable time asking the question, "What does God want me to do?" As happened with me a few years later, Lyn was led by the Spirit in choosing the pursuits she ended up pursuing.

Likewise, if you're a stay-at-home parent, you can utilize *The Jonah Factor* to discern new directions God may be prompting you toward, especially as your children grow older. The steps are almost identical to the ones laid out previously, and the leap of faith is no less dramatic than someone who might be leaving a fulltime job.

For the Student

Many students graduate from college with a degree in the field different from the one they had originally decided upon. In a sense, the college experience is heavily tied into discernment—to prepare for a lifetime. I changed directions four times in college before finally deciding to pursue a degree in journalism, which now I regard as more dumb luck than any particular wisdom on my part.

Unfortunately, many college students only follow the money, looking at which careers pay well or offer security, instead of pursuing a career where their gifts and abilities match their true "calling." Pursuing a well-paying career is not bad, as long as we recognize how we can serve God in that particular field. But too many students miss the opportunity to pursue vocations that would ultimately be more rewarding for them and more in line with God's call on their lives.

Regrettably, at many colleges there is no spiritual component to helping students decide which career is most appropriate. A college education is often more about preparing students to plug a hole in the workforce than trying to determine what they were uniquely built by God to do.

In that scenario *The Jonah Factor* provides an opportunity to step back and evaluate which career or field will best fulfill God's plan for the student.

For the Retiree

Growing numbers of retirees are looking for challenges they'll find fulfilling and that will keep their skills sharp. Increasingly, retirees who spent a lifetime in jobs that made them successful are looking for volunteer work or second careers that give their lives significance. After all, this is the period of life in which they hoped to take off the yoke of responsibility and replace it with the blessing of doing something more meaningful.

Spiritual discernment for the retiree should be more focused on the Grounding and Self-Evaluating Stages. Men, especially, often haven't taken the time to be discerning. For many of them, particularly from the World War II generation, earning a living was a primary concern. Everything else, including job satisfaction, took a back seat. Retirement provides the opportunity for them to reflect and seek God's will in whatever work they now take on.

Retirees today have a particular challenge in deciding what to spend their time on. They're healthier and more energetic, and there's a growing need for volunteers in hospitals, churches, nonprofit organizations, and government organizations. For most retirees, it's more a matter of when to say "no."

Discernment is especially important when we're bombarded with opportunities. However, *The Jonah Factor* needs to be altered slightly to be effective for the retiree.

For the Church or Community Volunteer

A number of Americans are what can be called "professional volunteers." They're people who have the financial resources that allow them to do whatever they want, and they've chosen to pour significant time and effort into volunteer activities. Like many retirees, they've achieved success; now they're looking for greater significance. Their endeavors transcend the activities we usually associate with volunteers, such as answering phones or stuffing envelopes. Many of them are on the boards of local nonprofits, serving on church councils and running community programs.

Increasingly, these volunteers are not retirees. Often, they're entrepreneurs who sold a business, employees at startups who sold their stock options, or people who have downsized their lifestyle sufficiently to take advantage of an inheritance or cashed out some home equity. Much like retirees, however, their greatest challenge is deciding what volunteer activities to engage in. Their success in life makes them attractive to churches, nonprofits, and community agencies that are looking for sharp, dedicated, and successful people to run programs, raise funds, or start new ministries.

Most of the steps in *The Jonah Factor* are appropriate for this group, with the possible exception of Step 7 (actively pursue opportunities). In many cases, trying out something new can be done in the context of the organization at which they're considering devoting their energies, instead of at a church.

The more difficult part comes when they feel led to do something else, perhaps for a different organization or ministry. The fact that they're already doing something worthwhile or important may prevent them from considering other opportunities more in line with a new direction God has in mind.

The Grounding Stage (Steps 1 and 2) is especially important here because it will help them discern whether God is releasing them from what they're currently doing and directing them to some other activity or ministry.

The Clergy or Others Engaged in Full-time Ministry

This is another tricky area. After all, men and women in the ministry are already doing what God has called them to do, aren't they? Perhaps not.

Those in full-time Christian ministry are susceptible to the same discernment dilemmas as everyone else, especially when it comes to hearing God's call to leave a position—or even a congregation.

I'm often reminded of that when I visit some churches. Whether at a wedding, funeral, or Sunday worship service, I'm often dumbstruck by the apathetic preaching and leading of services by those who God has called to ministry. All too many pastors, ministers, priests, and other worship leaders look bored, simply going through a routine they've probably repeated hundreds of times before. Surely they didn't begin their ministry like that.

Perhaps they haven't taken to heart the well-worn verse, "There is a time for everything, and season for every activity under heaven" (Ecclesiastes 3:1). It's especially appropriate for those in the ministry.

Although most of *The Jonah Factor* steps are appropriate for this group, some will be problematic, especially in the Trial Balloon Stage (Steps 6 and 7). It's one thing for a church member to try out something new that has the possibility of failing in his or her home church. But it's quite another thing, if you're clergy or a church staff member, to expect your congregation to continue to support you if you crash and burn on something that turns out wasn't the strength you thought it would be. For those who are in full-time ministry, this stage is probably best conducted elsewhere, perhaps at a different congregation or a different organization involved in the kind of ministry you feel you're being led toward.

Much like the volunteer, discussed earlier, those involved in full-time ministry should pay particular attention to the Grounding Stage (Steps 1 and 2) of *The Jonah Factor*. It's too easy to get caught up in the importance of what we're doing in ministry—not to mention the ego gratification that often comes with it—that we forget to keep coming back into the throne room of God to determine what new things God may have in mind for us.

As the verse in Ecclesiastes reminds us, ministries, like careers, have seasons. Even within the church, programs and ministries are not intended to last forever. Neither are the efforts of the people who run them. We need to be sensitive to God's calling, especially when we are being led to stop doing something, even when it's successful.

Reflection Point

Key thought

> The Jonah Factor *techniques are geared toward helping us
> determine our God-ordained vocation, including those of
> us engaged in less traditional jobs or careers.*

Questions

1. What is your particular unique situation (student, stay-at-home parent, volunteer, clergy member), and how do you see *The Jonah Factor* steps helping you discern God's calling in your life?

2. Which, if any, steps seem most important to you? Least important?

3. Do you know someone in yet another unique situation who might benefit from working through these steps? Invite them to get started.

CHAPTER ELEVEN

Five Deadly Excuses

We are the Borg. Resistance is futile.

Lower your shields and surrender your vessel.

We will add your own biological and

technical distinctiveness to our own.

Your culture will adapt to serve us.

—*From the movie* Star Trek: First Contact

IF YOU'RE A STAR TREK FAN, YOU KNOW OF THE BORG. They're creatures who roam the galaxy—space-age body snatchers of sorts—latching onto the hapless inhabitants of any spacecraft they encounter. In addition to changing the appearance of their victims, the Borg take over their minds. Fairly quickly, the victims become the Borg.

Unfortunately, that's similar to the way our culture can overwhelm us. Although we may intend to have our relationship with Christ dictate how we think and act, American mainstream culture exerts an incredibly strong influence, one that's difficult to resist.

It was this kind of challenge that prompted Paul to write, "Do not conform any longer to the pattern of this world, but be transformed by the renewing of your mind. Then you will be able to test and approve what God's will is—his good, pleasing, and perfect will" (Romans 12:2).

When we take our cues from the culture, we seek security, power, ego-gratification, prestige, and comfort—all things that get in the way of what Christ is trying to do within us. We cannot live the abundant life Jesus promises until we embrace him instead of the culture.

Don't underestimate the power of the culture to derail your attempts to pursue the purpose God intends for you in your work. Although *The Jonah Factor* is set up to help you tune out the cacophony of culture, it's still very difficult not to be affected by it. Most likely, there will be many temptations to abandon your plan, and they can show up in some of the following excuses.

Excuse #1: "It's Too Late for Me"

In a *Peanuts* comic strip, Lucy observes, "If you're not beguiling by age twelve, forget it." We chuckle at that, perhaps not realizing we often put the same absurd limits on ourselves and on God. Regardless of whether we're in our forties, fifties, or sixties, we can think we're stuck in our jobs. We focus on what we'll give up: income, perks, vacation time, retirement plans, and other benefits that we've worked hard and long to earn from our current employer. We tell ourselves, "If only I was younger, I could do this."

That mindset not only limits us, but it restricts God. Plus, it's not biblical.

Abraham was seventy-five years old when he and his wife picked up and moved. He was eighty-six when his first son was born, and one hundred when son number two came along. Moses was about eighty and his brother Aaron was eighty-three when they first confronted Pharaoh. Jacob was a whopping 130 when he picked up and moved his family to Egypt. And Noah was six hundred when he built the ark!

Granted, there's little chance any of us will live to be 130 or six hundred. The point is, however, that each of them trusted God in spite of their advanced age.

Most of us have heard the story about how Colonel Harland Sanders started his "finger-lickin' good" Kentucky Fried Chicken (now called KFC) franchise at the age of sixty-five. We figure that's an anomaly, however. We believe we could never do something like that at an age that's supposed to be consumed by travel, golf, and late-afternoon martinis. Old Colonel Sanders proved it's feasible to shift gears regardless of our age.

Plus, we have the promise of Luke 1:37, that "nothing is impossible with God."

Excuse #2: "I'm Afraid To"

This was part of Jonah's dilemma. He probably was fearful of what would happen to him if the terrible Ninevites got their hands on him. Or perhaps he was afraid that God really was as merciful as promised. His fear of the unknown prompted him to head in the other direction.

Fear is an understandable companion to *The Jonah Factor* participants. There will be times when you scratch your head, afraid that you might not really be hearing God's voice. In the midst of that fear and confusion, you do nothing.

That's where revisiting some of *The Jonah Factor*'s 13 Steps (especially Steps 1 and 2) can be helpful in reminding you of what God has specifically shown you along the way. Another way to address this concern is to keep a journal throughout the process, giving you something to re-examine and to jog your memory regarding the direction in which God is leading you. If you don't already have a journal, buy one. Or use the journal starting on page 178 of this book. Take notes on what you think God—or any others you enlist as part of the 13 Steps—is showing you.

In addition, your concern may be prompted by the fact that you've never attempted to trust God in even the small stuff. And now, preparing to take a leap of faith is really stretching it.

Years ago when I joined Toastmasters International, I did so not just to learn how to speak in public more effectively. I was scared to death to get up in front of an audience, so I was hoping to get rid of those darned butterflies that made me dread giving presentations.

Frankly, I never did get rid of those butterflies. They still make appearances every time I get up to speak in front of a group. However, through practice and prayer, I did finally teach them to fly in formation.

It's similar with *The Jonah Factor.* Abandoning ourselves to God's will is scary stuff that contradicts many of our assumptions about how we should be living our lives. It's like taking a step off a high dive for the first time. Jumping off a diving board so high above the waterline requires us to override the wiring that's intended to keep us alive. Our subconscious screams, "What, are you nuts? This is too high. You're going to get hurt." However, we override that innate fear with logic, telling ourselves that it's only water and that others who jumped before us survived the plunge. Then we jump.

That's why your congregation and other Christians are such important components in *The Jonah Factor.* In addition to surrounding you in prayer, they can show you tangible examples of people who have lived a life of faith that, although frightening at times, can be far more rewarding than one lived in the cocoon of safety. They'll help pump some courage into you and provide examples of people who jumped off the high dive and lived to talk about it.

Excuse #3: "I Don't Want To"

You may well get to Step 13 and decide to step back from the brink, choosing not to take a leap of faith. Why is that? After all, the preceding twelve steps are intended to help you build confidence in God and trust that God won't let you fall when you finally leap.

That may be due to fear, as seen in the previous section. However, it could also be caused by other factors, such as pride, the unwillingness to try something new, or trying to meet other people's expectations.

Pride is an especially persistent sin. Our reluctance to follow God's leading is often the result of our unwillingness to give up status, power, a big house, a comfortable lifestyle, or other things important to the ego. We might not be willing to make the necessary sacrifices. We often don't realize that's our motivation, telling ourselves that, as masters of our destiny, we simply choose not to leap.

Throughout *The Jonah Factor* process, it's important to keep in mind why you're on the ledge preparing to leap.

Remember, this is not necessarily about what you want, although the outcome will be wonderful because you'll be engaged in an occupation or activities consistent with what God created you for. You've been preparing for months—or even years—to get to this point. You know in your heart that it's the right decision.

Your "old Adam" (see chapter 12) will scream against the decision you're about to make. Continuously, the enemy known by many names (Satan, the devil) tries to trick us into believing that we alone have the power to create a fulfilling life and that we don't need God to make that happen. So, we're deceived into thinking that we can just back away from the ledge and get along just fine without having to follow the Lord's leading.

Resist the self-centeredness of this excuse and realize it's just another attempt to put you, not God, in the driver's seat of the decision.

Here's an analogy that might help: Among my favorite memories of growing up in New Jersey are of going sledding on winter nights. We would grab our sleds after dinner and head for a nearby hill. The hill was unlit, too dangerous to slide down on most winter nights. However, for a few nights each winter a full moon provided just enough light to allow us to do this safely. Here's the lesson in that homespun example: A full moon is only possible when the sun's rays aren't blocked by the earth and are allowed to hit the moon's surface. Just like I wasn't able to enjoy my favorite nighttime winter activity until the world got out of the way, we won't feel confident to take a leap of faith until WE get out of the way and allow God's purpose to shine fully onto our lives.

Excuse #4: "I'll Do It Some Day"

Church pews are filled with people who will serve God "some day." Their explanation usually starts out with "I'll serve God" and has a variety of endings, such as ". . . when I retire," ". . . when I win the lottery," ". . . when the kids move out" or ". . . when I have more time."

Frankly, most of us never reach the point where serving God will not involve some sacrifice of either time or prosperity. So we deceive ourselves into waiting until we think it will be more comfortable or convenient to do so.

By delaying that which we know we must do in God's kingdom, we deny God the best we can offer—such as our youth—and we miss out on the blessings God has in store.

Plus, for many of us, "some day" never comes.

Excuse #5: "I Don't Have Much to Serve God With"

When we think of serving God—especially in whatever work we do—we feel inadequate. Perhaps that goes back to the mistaken impression most of us have about who really is called to serve God (see chapter 6). We incorrectly believe that only "professional religious people" receive that kind of call.

As we've seen, pastors, ministers, and others involved in full-time ministry are not the only ones tapped to serve God in their vocations; we all are. That said, we often take an incorrect inventory of our talents and abilities and conclude that we don't have anything God would be interested in using, forgetting that God can take even a mustard seed (Matthew 13) and turn it into something huge.

Look at what Jesus did in Matthew 14 with a few fishes and several loaves of bread. It wasn't much, barely enough to feed the disciples who were accompanying Jesus that day. Jesus turned those meager offerings into food for thousands.

He can do the same with whatever skills, talents, and abilities we bring to him.

Reflection Point

Key thought

In this chapter, we've captured only five excuses that can interfere with our efforts to follow God's direction in the work we do. There are dozens of others that prevent us from achieving the satisfaction that comes from truly rewarding, God-ordained work. Don't look to our culture for direction. Instead, seek God's wisdom, and gradually you'll see that God has an answer to every excuse we might use.

Questions

1. What is preventing you from taking the leap of faith into the work that God wants you to do?

2. Picture yourself doing the work that *The Jonah Factor* stairway has led you toward. What do you see? How does it feel?

CHAPTER TWELVE

A Benediction

Commit to the LORD whatever you do,

and your plans will succeed.

—*Proverbs 16:3*

JONAH FELL VICTIM TO THE PERFECT STORM. He never saw it coming. By refusing to embrace the specific call God had placed on him, Jonah entered the vortex created when God's plans and human plans collide. He was rescued only after he relinquished control of his life to the God who had pursued him so relentlessly.

Perhaps you identify with Jonah. Although you can't quite put your finger on it, there's a malaise in your life, much of it centered on whatever work you do. You tell yourself, "It's just a job." Yet, so much of your time and efforts are wrapped into that work, and it impacts your life far beyond the hours you actually spend engaged in it.

Our work is intended to be done in partnership with our Lord. And, as in any partnership, both parties enter the relationship with certain expectations. God expects us to follow and promises to see us through any difficulties resulting from obeying God's call. Conversely, we can expect God to look out for us as we engage in the work God calls us to do.

Let me leave you with a thought. This gem comes from John Fischer, who is senior writer for *Purpose Driven Life Daily Devotionals* (www.purposedrivenlife.com). In an August 2005 e-mail devotion, he had a remarkable insight into the well-known account of Peter's walk on the water with Jesus, found in Matthew 14.

Mr. Fischer notes that Peter didn't decide by himself to climb out of the boat and join Jesus on top of the waves. Neither did Jesus simply call out to Peter and tell him to test the waters, so to speak.

Here's how the event unfolds: It is very early morning, probably around 3 a.m. The disciples are in the middle of a lake aboard a boat being tossed by wind and waves. In the darkness they spot Jesus walking toward them atop the waves. They're terrified, thinking they're seeing a ghost. But Jesus reassures them. Peter yells out, saying, "Lord, if it's you, tell me to come to you on the water" (Matthew 14:28). Jesus invites him, and Peter, indeed, walks on the water.

In his devotion, John Fischer keenly observes:

Notice Peter didn't ask if he could come; he asked Jesus to invite him to come. Actually that's pretty brilliant when you think about it. By asking Jesus to invite him, he is tying Jesus into the enterprise. If Jesus invites him to come, then Jesus is responsible for what might happen. Jesus isn't going to invite Peter to walk out to him if he didn't know he could do it, or save him if he couldn't.

That partnership is at the heart of *The Jonah Factor.* Throughout each of the 13 Steps, we're both asking God to invite us to do the work for which God has called us, and holding God responsible for what will happen along the way. We're trusting that God won't let us slip beneath the waves once we step off the boat.

I took that leap of faith on April 23, 2004, when I submitted a recommendation to my employer to eliminate my longtime position with the firm. At that moment I was transformed from Jonah stuck in the belly of the big fish to Peter walking on the water with Jesus. My faith has been tested unlike any other time in my life, and I've continuously had to trust that God wouldn't let me or my family slip beneath the waves. And Jesus has proven to me countless times that he is, indeed, trustworthy beyond our greatest expectations.

My wish is that you'll experience firsthand the amazement and awesome joy that results from finding the work that God has intended for you, now and through eternity.

I know that God will.

CHAPTER THIRTEEN

It's Your Turn

I never failed once.

It just happened to be a 2,000-step process.

—*Thomas Edison*

FAITHFUL READER, IT'S TIME FOR ME TO HAND THE PEN TO YOU.

Use the following pages to record thoughts, inspirations, and whatever you think God is showing you about the work he wants to direct you toward. Jot some ideas down (especially as you engage in Steps 1 and 2) and come back to these pages frequently as you progress along *The Jonah Factor* steps. As you go through those steps, record your revelations in the journal starting on page 178. See which ideas persist and which ones you can build upon. Pay special attention to impressions, thoughts, and Bible verses that keep coming to mind. Cross out those that pop up once or twice and then go away.

Perhaps you will discover that you're already doing the work to which God has called you. Or maybe it's finally time for you to be freed from the belly of the big fish.

Within the journal that follows, enter the most important thoughts and impressions that occur to you as you engage in each of the steps. Continue to narrow down those thoughts as you ascend the stairway, leading toward greater discernment of the work that God has waiting for you. Pay particular attention to recurring thoughts as you progress up the stairway.

The Jonah Factor® Journal

The Grounding Stage

Step 1: Pray

_____

_____
_____
_____
_____
_____
_____
_____
_____
_____
_____
_____

The Grounding Stage
• • • • • • • • • • • •
Step 2: Meditate on scripture

_____

_____

_____

_____

_____

_____

_____

_____

_____

_____

_____

The Self-Evaluating Stage
• • • • • • • • • • • • •
Step 3: Examine your passions

_____

_____

_____

_____

_____

_____

_____

_____

_____

_____

_____

The Self-Evaluating Stage
. . . .
Step 4: Consider your talents

_____

_____

_____

_____

_____

_____

_____

_____

_____

_____

_____

The Self-Evaluating Stage
. . . .
Step 5: Evaluate your current job

_____

_____

_____

_____

_____

_____

_____

_____

_____

_____

_____

The Trial Balloon Stage
• • • • • • • • • • • •
Step 6: Commit to a congregation

_____

_____

_____

_____

_____

_____

_____

_____

_____

_____

_____

The Trial Balloon Stage
• • • • • • • • • • • •
Step 7: Actively pursue opportunities

_____

_____

_____

_____

_____

_____

_____

_____

_____

_____

_____

The Learning Stage
• • • • • • • • • • •
Step 8: Learn new things

_____

_____

_____

_____

_____

_____

_____

_____

_____

_____

_____

The Confirming Stage
• • • • • • • • • • • •
Step 9: Build a team of consultants

_____

_____

_____

_____

_____

_____

_____

_____

_____

_____

_____

The Confirming Stage
· · · · · · · · · · · · ·
Step 10: Seek confirmation

_____

_____

_____

_____

_____

_____

_____

_____

_____

_____

_____

_____

The Testing Stage
· · · · · · · · · ·
Step 11: Put out the fleece

_____

_____

_____

_____

_____

_____

_____

_____

_____

_____

_____

_____

The Testing Stage
· · · · · · · · · ·
Step 12: Be Faithful in small things

_____
_____
_____
_____
_____
_____
_____
_____
_____
_____
_____

The Final Stage
· · · · · · · · · ·
Step 13: Take the leap of faith

_____
_____
_____
_____
_____
_____
_____
_____
_____
_____
_____

Acknowledgments

Therefore encourage one another and build each other up,

just as in fact you are doing.

—*1 Thessalonians 5:11*

THIS BOOK WAS MADE POSSIBLE BY COUNTLESS PEOPLE WHO TOOK THIS VERSE TO HEART.

My deepest gratitude goes to Lyn, my wife and life partner for more than twenty-seven years. She has trusted in God and believed in me far beyond what I ever imagined or could have expected. The prayers and partnership of my children, Matthew and Hannah, were also critical in this adventure of a lifetime.

I had many enthusiastic supporters as I engaged, sometimes tentatively, in the steps that became *The Jonah Factor*. They included my mother Waltraud Klodt, father-in-law Wink Martindale, his wife, Sandy, and my mother-in-law Madelyn Dale.

I was blessed with amazing encouragement from my congregation, Ascension Lutheran Church in Thousand Oaks, and its pastors over the past fifteen years: Tim Delkeskamp, Willis Moerer, Larry Wagner, and Howard Wennes. These men have been powerful examples of God's love, grace, and encouragement. Special thanks to Howie for opening doors into publishing that seemed tightly nailed shut.

Members of my Tuesday morning Men's Bible Study group, led by Mark Winter, were instrumental in helping me think through how to make this book valuable for people from different walks of life. They became my first focus group to determine if *The Jonah Factor* could have a broader application for others. The prayers and support of my Tuesday evening Bible Study group, of which I've been a member for more than a dozen years, were also critical.

Priscilla MacRae provided a second focus group of sorts by allowing me to use *The Jonah Factor* as I consulted on a Pepperdine University research study she was conducting.

Dan McMaster provided invaluable manuscript critique and godly wisdom whenever I wavered in my commitment to follow God's call. Incredibly, God brought Bill Vietinghoff, a former associate of mine from more than twenty years ago, back into my life to help me figure out how to bypass rejection slips and get this book published.

My professors and the library staff at Fuller Theological Seminary continue to amaze me with their knowledge and help me uncover the context and meaning of the more veiled verses of Scripture.

Special thanks go to Augsburg Fortress, Publishers. Beth Lewis, its president, took a Step 13 leap of faith and said yes to this book. Scott Tunseth, my editor, provided skilled first aid for the manuscript and edited it with a sharp but gentle scalpel. I am in his debt. Michelle Cook's wonderful design transformed words on paper into something remarkably easy to read. And Bob Todd, already busier than a Doberman at a flea convention, gave this book his time and talent to ensure its success in the marketplace.

And, as this book's most significant contributor, my hope is that *The Jonah Factor* brings glory to God, whose inspiration was critical throughout the time in which I researched and wrote it. To God be the glory—now and forever. Amen!

About the Author

ED KLODT (last name rhymes with "boat") is the editor and publisher of *Digging Deeper,* a syndicated publication of daily devotions distributed weekly throughout the United States (www.diggingdeeper.com).

A self-described "Jonah" for many years, Ed has been a senior manager of communications at several Fortune 500 firms. In 2004, after having developed and implemented *The Jonah Factor's* 13 Steps, Ed left the corporate world to pursue God's call of developing a national writing and speaking ministry aimed at helping people discern their God-given vocation.

A popular speaker at a variety of churches, retreats, and seminars, Ed has been a lay minister for sixteen years and was a two-term president at the 2,500-member Ascension Lutheran Church in Thousand Oaks, California. He is also an adult education instructor, with a particular focus on helping people understand biblical concepts and apply them to everyday life.

At the time of the book's publication, he is working toward a Masters degree in Theology at Fuller Theological Seminary. He and his wife, Lyn, have two children and two pups.

For additional resources and information visit:
www.jonahfactor.com

Or contact the author at:
The Jonah Factor®
1534 North Moorpark Road, #118
Thousand Oaks, CA 91360-5129

More praise for *The Jonah Factor*

"Martin Luther taught us about vocation, Rick Warren touched a cultural nerve by addressing purpose, and now Ed Klodt in *The Jonah Factor* integrates vocation and purpose as he addresses our occupational search for meaning. Klodt, a seasoned veteran in business and a fellow traveler in the search for God's will for our lives, holds up Jonah like a mirror. We see ourselves and our folly in ignoring God's call to serve in daily life, and we wake up to the Spirit's disturbing call to honor God in, with, and under our daily chores."
 —*Howie Wennes, Interim President*
 California Lutheran University

"A friend of mine once observed that Americans are people who worship their work, work at their play, and play at their worship. Our generation has raised professional life to a position of prominence, while making plans to escape from it at their earliest opportunity. Christians in our culture have seldom worked with a better formula than their non-faithed peers in sorting out the search for the 'perfect job.' Thank heaven for Ed Klodt's thoughtful work in *The Jonah Factor*. May God's voice now be heard as Christians evaluate anew their commitment to one of life's most important roles. Career is what you're paid for, but calling is what you're made for. Christians who are pursuing their calling have the ability to change the world!"
 —*Bob Shank, Founder/CEO, The Master's Program*

"*The Jonah Factor* is a very readable, user-friendly book which invites the reader into discovering one's vocation and meaningful life and work. The author draws upon his life experience, biblical references, and other resources to assist in this journey. It reads as though it is a close friend, a companion on the way and, as such, I will want to keep it close by as an ongoing source of reflection and guidance."
 —*Bud Holland, Coordinator, Office for Ministry Development,*
 The Episcopal Church Center

"For the large number of workers not finding job satisfaction but feeling caught, *The Jonah Factor* provides a way out through practical and easy-to-follow steps."
—*Jim Gingerich, Coordinator, Mennonite Men*

"*The Jonah Factor* is a valuable resource for any church that is finding a ministry with those in their congregations who are seeking fulfillment in all the areas of their life. It provides a blueprint for moving from having a job to fulfilling a calling. It presents a plan for moving from 'job hunting' to engaging in a spiritual journey to find a new identity as servants of God. It is a call to rediscover the foundations of the Christian community."
—*Dr. Curtis A. Miller, Past President of the North American Conference of Church Men's Staff and Former Associate of Men's Ministries, Presbyterian Church (USA)*

"As a retired U. S. army colonel who loved my job, I wondered, 'What could I possibility learn from reading a book that will assist me through 13 Spiritual Steps to Finding the Job of a Lifetime?' It did not take long for me to realize that much of the material provided was not only most valuable to those individuals looking for the job of a lifetime, but for those people, like myself, who have volunteer jobs as well.

"With the turmoil in the job market today, with retirement plans being totally changed, the lack of company and employee loyalty, and changing of jobs more frequently, I highly recommend this book be read by all individuals (male and female) who are unhappy in their jobs and are contemplating a move."
—*Floyd M. Gilbert, Colonel U. S. Army (Retired) President, National Council of Presbyterian Men, Presbyterian Church (USA)*

"Human nature resists getting outside the comfort zones, but *The Jonah Factor* faces the fear/faith factors squarely and gives the reader a full tool-box for mining the riches found in Scriptures and in the aptitudes God has given each of us. In twenty years facilitating group ministry to ten thousand persons in job transition, I've met many who could be blessed by Ed Klodt's book, including me!"
—*Pastor Rod Anderson, St. Andrew Lutheran Church and Job Transition Group, Eden Prairie, Minnesota*

"A Christian's calling is to serve God and humanity in family and community roles, in church roles, and in one's employment. *The Jonah Factor* focuses on the latter aspect of vocation—the job. This book is written for people who may wonder whether their present job is the best place for them to serve God and God's people. One can serve in almost any work, but sometimes it is faithful to consider whether a change is advisable and necessary. This book can aid in discerning."

    —Stanley N. Olson, Executive Director for Vocation
     and Education, Evangelical Lutheran Church in America

"I confess that I am usually not one who enjoys or appreciates books that are titled something like, *10 Ways to Succeed* or *12 Ways to Make God Love You.* Sorry, but to me, life is not that simple. However, in saying that, let me also confess that *The Jonah Factor: 13 Spiritual Steps to Finding the Job of a Lifetime* is a helpful, practical, and realistic guide that can enable the reader to sort out, seek, and be supportive to those of us who continue to search for God's will in our lives."

    —Rich Bimler, Past President, Wheat Ridge Ministries

"At its core, faith is a quest for meaning that begins and ends in God our Creator. How we make a living often impedes our quest. In *The Jonah Factor,* Ed Klodt has combined many tried-and-tested roads into one, systematic pathway for those restless-spirit folks coming aware of God's call to make the journey from 'making a living' to 'living out one's making.'"

    —J. Gregory Alexander, Acting Regional Minister,
     Christian Church in Kentucky

"The principles outlined in this book will be a great resource for anyone discerning his/her vocation. As a leader of the church called to help indentify gifts and walk alongside of young people, I wecome specific practices like the ones in *The Jonah Factor* to help guide their sense of vocation and what it means to be part of the Kingdom of God."

    —Rev. Sean L. Forde, ELCA Young Men's Ministry Specialist

"God wants a radical win-win life for each of us, and if we all followed the kind of discernment found in *The Jonah Factor,* our world would be a much different place!"

    —Dianha Ortega-Ehreth, Associate Director for Youth Leadership and
  Spiritual Formation, Evangelical Lutheran Church in America